AFRICAN CHILDREN IN PERIL

THE WEST'S TOXIC LEGACY

AFRICAN CHILDREN IN PERIL

THE WEST'S TOXIC LEGACY

Brian Waller

Copyright © 2023 Brian Waller

The moral right of the author has been asserted.

Apart from any fair dealing for the purposes of research or private study, or criticism or review, as permitted under the Copyright, Designs and Patents Act 1988, this publication may only be reproduced, stored or transmitted, in any form or by any means, with the prior permission in writing of the publishers, or in the case of reprographic reproduction in accordance with the terms of licences issued by the Copyright Licensing Agency. Enquiries concerning reproduction outside those terms should be sent to the publishers.

Matador
Unit E2 Airfield Business Park,
Harrison Road, Market Harborough,
Leicestershire. LE16 7UL
Tel: 0116 279 2299
Email: books@troubador.co.uk
Web: www.troubador.co.uk/matador
Twitter: @matadorbooks

ISBN 978 1803136 547

British Library Cataloguing in Publication Data.
A catalogue record for this book is available from the British Library.

Printed and bound in the UK by TJ Books Limited, Padstow, Cornwall
Typeset in 11.5pt Jensen Pro by Troubador Publishing Ltd, Leicester, UK

Matador is an imprint of Troubador Publishing Ltd

Contents

Acknowledgements	ix
Preface	xi
Introduction	xiii

Section 1: Children in Peril – facts and causes   1

1 The predicament of children in sub-Saharan Africa (SSA) – poverty, malnutrition, poor health, and extraordinary levels of infant mortality   3

2 What must have been the underlying causes of such widespread disadvantages and difficulties?   19

Section 2: Western interventions in SSA   27

3 The legacy of the Atlantic Slave trade for African families and children   29

4 Colonialism and its damaging social and economic impact on African families and children   46

5 Neo-Colonialism –'The last stage of Imperialism'   80

6 The failure of Tropical Medicine to help vulnerable African children   85

7 The missed opportunity; the World Bank's failure to develop primary health care in Africa and the long-term price paid by Africa's children   95

8 Neoliberalism and its destructive impact on children's health and well-being in Africa   113

Section 3: The impact of these events on children and what must happen next   127

9 How have these events, together, affected African children?   129

10 How is Africa already responding?	135
11 What must be done now to help Africa's children?	144

References 160

Acknowledgements

In writing this book, I am indebted to my many colleagues and friends in Africa, including Anne Hart, Marksen Wafula Masinde, Charles Mugasa, Garry Ion (CMS), Msgr. Thomas Kisembo, Dr Gwaita Aggrey and the very many marvellous volunteers working within Home-Start to help parents. Thanks, too, to Dr Sheila Shinman, Evi Hatzivarnava, Stewart Jeffrey, Prof Raphael Kaplinsky, Sheena Stewart, Chair of Trustees at Home-Start Worldwide, Wenche Heimholt Isaachsen and Dr Lata Narayanaswamy at the School of Politics and International Studies at Leeds University, for their support and invaluable encouragement. I thank them all, but I take full responsibility for all the views and comments I have expressed here. Without my wife, Denise's endlessly patient and sympathetic support, I could not have even started to undertake the work involved in researching and writing this book.

I want to thank all the photographers who took the pictures included here. I have tried to ensure that they have been used respectfully and in context to illuminate and emphasise the narrative. In particular, I thank Istock for permitting me to use the map of Africa, and Alamy for permitting me to use the photographs of two boys in Malawi, of Stanley meeting Livingstone, of Harewood House, of Halfdan Mahler, of the Berlin conference 1885, and of the Lever Brothers washing advertisement. I thank Anti-Slavery International UK for the photograph taken in 1904 by one of their missionaries of the Congolese worker with the severed foot and leg of his child. And I thank SuSanA Secretariat for their photograph of the small child playing by a dirty stream in Kampala, highlighting their work in bringing clean water, sanitation and hygiene to many communities in sub-Saharan Africa. And, not least, I thank Gloria for allowing me to photograph her and her family in at her home near Fort Portal in Western Uganda.

Preface

The trigger for this book came from recent meetings with families with young children in villages in rural Western Uganda. Through my involvement with a charity, Home-Start Uganda, I had long been concerned about why so many infant children died in Uganda and across sub-Saharan Africa (SSA).

If current trends continue, 28.4 million children under 5s will die in SSA between 2020 and 2030, over 55% of all global infant deaths (Black et al., *The Lancet*, Feb. 2022).[1]

I wanted to talk with parents to ask them about this and find out how it affected their lives.

What I saw and learned from them has shaken me to the core. The profound poverty and despair that was so apparent in all of these families brought me to tears. Most had lost at least one child due to malnutrition and illnesses such as measles, diarrhoea, and malaria, all of which could have been treated or prevented. Mothers headed almost all of the families. The fathers had died or were absent for various reasons, sometimes because they had abandoned their wives or gone away to look for work. It was apparent that none of the families or their children had enough to eat, and they survived – that being precisely the right word – on a diet mainly comprised of leaves and roots. A few kept chickens, but they kept the eggs for sale to buy other food items at the local market. All lived in very rudimentary houses, without furniture, and none had proper latrines. Their children were dressed in rags, and their fathers hardly figured in their lives. Apart from the advice at antenatal clinics, none of these mothers or their children had any contact with health services. This is the reality, in 2022, of the so-called 'Third World'. It could have been a different planet.

One of the most disturbing aspects of this was that all of the villages where I met the families were within two miles of Fort Portal, one of Uganda's larger towns, an attractive and prosperous tourist centre with upmarket hotels and restaurants and a regional hospital. The local district, Kabarole, is often referred to as 'Uganda's breadbasket', and trucks of fresh food leave from there every day for the food markets of Uganda's capital. Other profitable crops, including tea and coffee, are grown in the area and end up in Western supermarkets. But all these families were desperately impoverished. Their lives and prospects and those of their children couldn't be more different than anywhere in the West. That is just not acceptable now or at any time – and the reasons for their awful predicament must be explained and made more widely known and acknowledged, however painful it might be.

Recent doctoral-level research has allowed me to appreciate the full extent of and facts about poverty, ill health, child malnutrition and mortality across sub-Saharan Africa and explore the immense gulf between the lives and prospects of African families, children, and their counterparts in the affluent West. I do not, though, want to limit this book in explaining how this calamity has come about, vital as it is to do that. Its chief purpose is to look at how it can be guaranteed that the next generation doesn't have to face the terrible but all too familiar prospect of being malnourished or fatally afflicted by diseases that could be prevented or treated.

It has been quite a challenge to write such a wide-ranging but relatively concise account of Africa's experience of Western interventions and the effects these have had on the subcontinent's children. I believe that I have the experience and qualifications to have undertaken it. My entire professional life has been spent working with families and children. But most significantly, I have worked with families with young children in Africa for decades.

Introduction

Thousands of books, articles and research papers have been written about sub-Saharan Africa's eventful history, particularly its fraught engagement with the West. They range from the diaries of celebrated missionaries such as David Livingstone to more recent analyses of Africa's prospects in the global economy.

At the end of the nineteenth century, the major Western powers unilaterally decided to divide the continent between them. For centuries, western powers, including Great Britain, Spain, and Portugal, were deeply involved in the enslavement and transhipment of Africans to work in the sugar plantations of the Caribbean. That era continues to produce books that, even today, reveal new and controversial evidence about how it finally became illegal in Britain and the British Empire in 1833.

The subsequent process of colonisation lasted well into the latter half of the twentieth century until all the colonised African nations became independent. It produced yet more accounts of how its impact had varied, country by country and widely varying descriptions of how well or badly foreign settlers and European governments had treated their colonial peoples over the preceding decades.

Even independence did not end the flow of books, articles, and research papers written about the post-colonial era in Africa. In particular, the politics of Sub-Saharan Africa have continued to be a source of great interest to the rest of the world.

But remarkably, and in the face of so much comment about Western involvement in Africa, little has been written about this has affected Africa's children. It has been too easy to take children for granted as few have ever had any voice, let alone agency, and their histories are almost unrecorded. The heartbreaking stories of today's parents and the alarming predictions mentioned earlier about the future of African children's health and well-being strongly suggest that very little attention has ever been directed to their welfare. This book must be one of the first to describe and evaluate the effect that Western interventions in Africa have had on them. It will be judged, too, on whether it offers practical ideas about how the wealthier nations, and especially the UK, can now assist the countries that they exploited for so many centuries

Section One

Children in Peril – Facts and Causes

Map of Africa

Chapter 1

The predicament of children in sub-Saharan Africa (SSA) – poverty, malnutrition, poor health and high levels of infant mortality

Sub-Saharan Africa is a large and geographically diverse region mainly comprised of small countries, except for Nigeria, South Africa and Ethiopia, which have larger populations, and Sudan and DR Congo, which are much larger geographically.

This southern part of Africa is one of the wealthiest regions in the world, measured by the extent of its reserves of scarce and precious minerals, including gold, diamonds, bauxite, uranium, copper and cobalt. It also has deposits of coltan, a precious mineral used in modern telecommunications equipment, including high-end phones, used widely in the rest of the world. Although threatened by global climate changes, it has a climate that allows a wide variety of food and other crops to be grown.

However, the wealth associated with these mineral reserves and vast natural resources, including tropical forests and wildlife, much envied and admired in the West, stands in complete contrast to the poverty and ill-health experienced by most of its citizens, especially by its children.

Across this enormous region, there are more than 500 million children and 150 million children under five years old. The facts about their circumstances and prospects are almost beyond belief and bear no relationship to the plentiful natural assets which exist across the subcontinent.

More than a third of them are seriously malnourished, starving, or developmentally damaged. There is a direct and clear connection between malnutrition and child deaths, which amounts to more than 25,000 preventable under-five deaths in the region every day – over 1000 deaths every hour – as a specific consequence. By any token, this is an enormous humanitarian disaster.

Although, according to the World Health Organisation (WHO), the World Bank (WB) and UNICEF, mortality rates have decreased over the last two decades, the 2021 mortality rate for under-fives in sub-Saharan Africa stood at 72 per thousand live births per annum. This is, on average, sixteen times higher than in Western Europe and higher than that in many parts of the region. For example, infant mortality rates in Nigeria are currently thirty times higher than in Britain.

What can possibly explain this huge discrepancy? What seismic events must have occurred in sub-Saharan Africa that might have been the cause of such enormous and shocking differences between this region and every country in the northern hemisphere? If such levels of child poverty, hunger and avoidable deaths existed in the West, national governments would face immense public pressure to urgently find explanations and remedies, just as happened during the recent Covid pandemic or when HIV/AIDS was feared as a global existential threat. Whilst there are plenty of contemporary references to the plight of Africa's children, its underlying causes have received far less attention. Many writers and Western politicians have been quick to blame African leaders for their greed and the corrupt governance of their new nations. These accusations are certainly not entirely invalid, and corruption exists in many African countries. But does it exist on such a scale as to be the primary cause of the extraordinary levels of poverty, disease, malnutrition and mortality across entire populations? Yet others – perhaps most Westerners – seem to think these have always been a feature – a 'given' of African life. The outdated picture of the primitive savage in many films and books shows how many Europeans still view Africans.

However, another much more feasible explanation for the plight of African children needs to be examined. It is about how the West has persistently subjugated and exploited Africa and its people over the centuries. I will show irrefutable evidence about how this has caused enormous disadvantages for African children. I don't suggest that any individuals, companies or foreign governments consciously decided to harm children. But in their remorseless thirst for African land and natural, mineral and human resources and easy profits, whether as invaders, colonisers, or businessmen, they have always regarded the injury caused to millions of children simply as 'collateral damage'.

Much research about child poverty, ill-health, malnutrition and deaths has focused on recent decades and hasn't questioned how such severe disadvantage has historically come about. Whatever the reasons, the shortage of literature about the underlying causes is extraordinarily concerning. How can such an extensive and deeply rooted tragedy have come about without it being the subject of far more detailed attention? The truth is that revelations about the reality of foreign interventions in Africa are now proving to be both painful and highly embarrassing to present-day governments. Some, including the United Kingdom, are very reluctant to admit to the facts of their often brutal involvement with Africa.

However contentious it might be to examine its historical causes, much more still needs to be done to highlight what they were and make them widely known. Indeed, not doing this can place governments in the invidious position of defending the indefensible. Recent examples of this can be seen in how badly the issue of how the statue of a notorious slaver was handled in Bristol and how the thoughtless 2022 Royal visit to the Caribbean produced an adverse reaction from the island governments there, who are contemplating breaking their links with the UK.

This book is an attempt to start to do just that. It is not intended to replace the work of the many scholars and researchers who have looked in detail at specific aspects of Africa's history. It should offer an accessible overview of why and how African families and children have become so impoverished and the connection between Western interventions and the extremely high levels of child malnutrition, child health and infant mortality across the region.

These most recent WHO, WB and UNICEF statistics graphically demonstrate the widespread and appalling extent of this for children in sub-Saharan Africa:

- **Children in sub-Saharan Africa (SSA) have the lowest expectation of life globally, at 62 and 65, respectively, for boys and girls (around 15 years less than their counterparts in Europe or North America)**
- The five countries in the world with the highest chance of children dying – Chad, the Central African Republic, Sierra Leone, Nigeria, and Mali – are all in SSA.
- The ten countries in the world with the highest child malnutrition levels are in SSA, except for Yemen and Haiti.
- The ten poorest countries in the world, except Afghanistan, are all in SSA.
- The twenty countries with the greatest chance of children dying from malnutrition are all in SSA.

- The ten countries with the highest maternal death rates are in sub-Saharan Africa (with rates more than one hundred times greater than those in Europe).
- The fifteen countries with the highest death rates for children under five are all in SSA.

These figures powerfully show the enormous concentration of disadvantage across a wide range of indicators of poverty, malnutrition and deaths affecting children in sub-Saharan Africa, especially in comparison to Europe and North America.

What explanations can there be for such gross differences to have come about?

The largely preventable deaths of more than a million infants every year can only be described as a catastrophe. It involves a prodigious loss of potential for the region, is economically and socially damaging for all its countries, and is grievously sad for their parents and families. And how can it have been so widely overlooked? With such enormous numbers of child deaths yearly, it's as if the rest of the world has been saying, 'African Children's Lives Don't Matter.'

Thankfully, there are positive responses to the appeals for funds when urgent and unmissable humanitarian crises involve starving children, such as those in Afghanistan, Syria and Yemen. But we seem much less troubled by the sheer scale of infant mortality caused by widespread chronic poverty, ill-health and malnutrition.

What is deeply troubling is that these extraordinarily high and persistent levels of infant malnutrition and related deaths in SSA are accepted as 'normal'. These are deaths that now hardly ever occur in the Northern hemisphere countries. Why should that be? Why should such appalling problems continue to exist anywhere in this increasingly prosperous and materialistic world full of scientific and medical innovations, technology, and international travel and tourism? And why are they concentrated in such huge numbers across southern Africa?

This hasn't been an accident, coincidence, or natural circumstances. And neither is it because Africans are lazy or genetically incompetent compared to people in the West. These reasons are often used as explanations – but they are entirely spurious. What has always struck me when working and travelling in Africa is the sheer industry and energy shown by people, whether farmers, teachers, foresters, engineers, highly skilled artisans, or artists. Some African leaders, such as Presidents Mobutu, Amin, and Zuma, have been venal and corrupt. Others have ruled dictatorially, but this can't have been the prime cause of such extraordinarily high numbers of child deaths even in their own countries. Much larger forces must have been involved in the exploitation and immiseration across most of an entire continent, the world's second-largest landmass and containing more scarce and precious mineral resources than any other part of the globe.

Many of the countries in SSA, although by no means all, currently have fertile soils and favourable climates for growing both food crops such as maize, rice, millet, cassava, sweet potatoes, grapes, and other fruits, and cash crops including sugar, cotton, cocoa, tea, and coffee. Some, including Kenya, Uganda, and Rwanda, grow highly profitable new crops such as chia and sesame seed, flowers and specialist teas and coffees, which all sell at high prices in the West. So why are the countries of sub-Saharan Africa, almost without exception, net food importers, and why is hunger still so widespread there?

A recent study[2] has warned that the impact of climate change will be far more severe in its effect on children in the poorer countries of the world than in the developed nations, whose wealth could make it possible to pay for and construct mitigation schemes, for example, to prevent flooding or desertification. Valuable crops such as coffee and tea cultivated at higher altitudes are already proving more challenging to grow in East Africa as average temperatures rise, which can only worsen due to climate change. Covid 19 has also disproportionately affected people in Africa, where vaccines have been much less available than in the West and health services generally are more rudimentary for most citizens. It has caused many families to become poorer due to higher levels of employment and the absence of any form of social protection such as those widely available in wealthier countries.

We also need to ask how these alarmingly high levels of child malnutrition and related and avoidable deaths have persisted, especially when Wasting, the most common form of malnutrition in southern African countries, can now be successfully treated. No one factor can adequately explain this. Over many years, it has almost certainly happened by the cumulative impact of critical but seemingly unconnected events and missed opportunities. Some, such as slavery and colonialism, are considered 'historical' – and no longer relevant. But, as will become apparent, all have left indelible and damaging scars on the region's current economic, social and cultural environments. I want to look more specifically at the effect that the West's past and present actions and policies have had on the well-being of African children. But before doing that, it makes sense to find out more about malnutrition itself and understand its principal causes and effects.

What is Malnutrition?

It is now accepted that children everywhere need to be well-nourished throughout their lives, both right from conception and then throughout their childhoods if they are to grow and develop properly. That includes their physical, emotional and intellectual development. It also means that mothers need to be well-nourished, especially during pregnancy. This understanding is the basis for how parents right across Europe and North America now try to treat their children and why maternal nourishment is seen as vital.

In *Explaining Child Development in Developing Countries*, two highly respected epidemiologists – Lawrence Haddad and Lisa Smith – have analysed child malnutrition in poorer nations, and especially in SSA.[3] They provide crucial evidence about its causes and suggestions about what needs to be done. They point, in particular, to four critical issues that explain why child malnutrition has continued to rise in SSA when levels have decreased in other poor regions. They are;

- *Insufficient levels of food availability*
- *Inadequate levels of education for girls and women*
- *Increases in levels of poverty*
- *The inferior status of women*

These factors were probably never even considered by colonial-era researchers, who appear to have allowed their pre-formed prejudices to dominate their thinking about the causes of child nutrition. That period will be examined later.

There is a risk, even now, of oversimplification. However, it is now generally agreed that child malnutrition falls into two broad types – Wasting and Stunting.[4]

Wasting, otherwise known as Severe Acute Malnutrition (SAM), is the most common form of acute and highly dangerous malnutrition that develops over relatively short periods – weeks or months – when children are markedly short of adequate nutrition. It occurs most commonly in famines and civil wars where children may be starving for different reasons. There could be

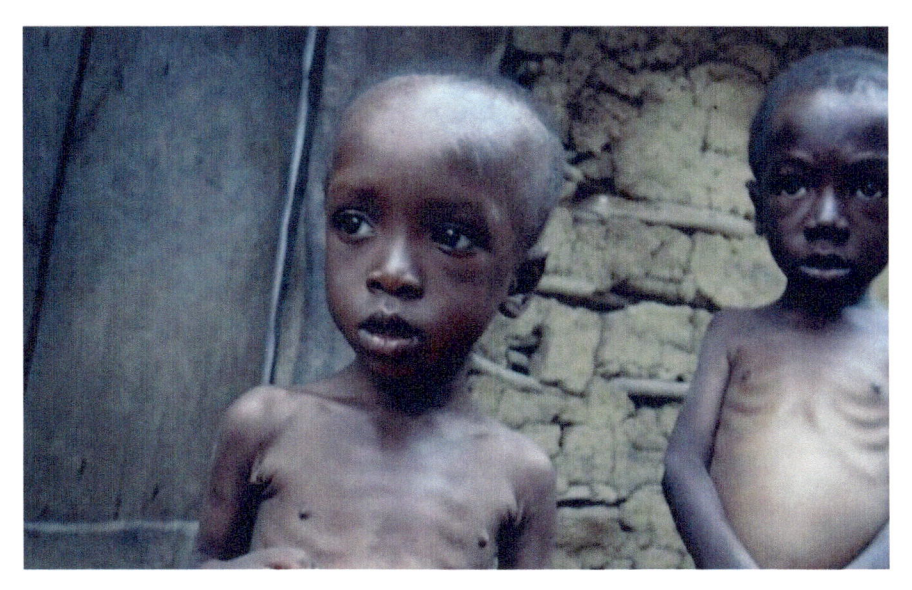

Wasted Children

other circumstances where this might happen, for example, in dysfunctional families or communities where, for some reason, there is an acute shortage of food or where families are desperately poor.

Wasting leads to very familiar signs of starvation. Children are underweight with distended abdomens and prominent ribs, sadly too familiar in photographs of children caught up in war zones or during urgent food shortages.

Right across SSA, about 15 per cent of children suffer from Wasting. This is a figure which needs careful interpretation. It is a regional average, but because occurrences are usually localised, the rates can be far higher than in the places where it happens. It often requires large-scale and urgent interventions. For too long, severe acute malnutrition was the only form of malnutrition to receive attention from researchers. For decades their investigations even into this one condition proved wholly inadequate. Various unlikely theories were followed about the underlying causes of Wasting until it became clear that the chief reason was insufficient food – simple starvation. Before this was adequately recognised, scientists looked at numerous other possibilities ranging from protein deficiency, excess of carbohydrates, deficiencies of fat, shortage of antioxidants, rare element deficiencies, the presence of mycotoxins, and free radical damage. During the mid-twentieth century, various groups and commercial interests pursued these improbable and even more bizarre ideas.

For years the predominant but ridiculous belief was that children suffered malnutrition because of 'protein deficiency' to such a point when, in 1955, the United Nations established a Protein Advisory Group (PAG) to close 'the protein gap' between rich and developing nations.[5] This idea was pursued in several African countries for decades. British Petroleum began manufacturing Single-Cell-Proteins grown on oil at one stage. Another product – Chlorella – was actually grown on sewage and is still sold as a health food in South Africa. Another development was the sales and marketing of breast milk substitutes for mothers' milk. Nestle's unethical marketing scandalously involved their sales staff dressing as nurses to persuade African mothers that factory-made products were superior to natural breast milk. Dr Cicely Williams described this episode as 'Tantamount to Murder.'[6]

Western companies' dubious influence was so potent that PAG, even as recently as 1973, advised that it was important for developing countries to have infant formula milk sources, even as in Africa, where breastfeeding was the accepted and widely practised norm.

Eventually, the protein theory was discredited as scientists looked more carefully at the evidence. The episode is often described as the 'Great Protein Fiasco', which can be seen as another manifestation of 'Tropical Medicine', frequently based on prejudiced and ignorant views about Africa (Jennifer Tappan).[7] Other odd ideas took its place, chief among them being the Malthusian-based theory that African malnutrition was essentially a product of overpopulation. The colonial view was that Africa's problems had arisen through its citizens' fault rather than anything to do with the West's actions. This was an astonishing step, given Africa's earlier massive depopulations due to slavery and colonial regimes such as those in Congo, where abusive labour practices had halved local population levels. However, such considerations did not prevent organisations, including the International Planned Parenthood Federation (IPPF), from setting up birth control clinics across Africa in the 1950s and subsequent American and British government aid programmes to African countries being made conditional for years on their adoption of family planning measures.

In a reflective paper. *'How little progress?'* (2018) British researcher John Nott[8] argues that Western concerns about African population growth after independence might have interfered with their development efforts. He states that Western attitudes to nutrition *'problematized fertility rather than social or economic inequality or inequitable food distribution.'*

Nott suggests that the family size issue is more complicated than organisations like IPPF thought. Couples everywhere make decisions about their families' size based on cultural, religious, and economic factors and health and longevity expectations. This is, and was, just as true in Africa as elsewhere – a fact not appreciated or understood by Western governments or organisations in the past or even now. Nott also suggests that in recent decades the Africanisation and feminisation of public health services have brought more informed decision-making into policymaking than when foreign agencies were only too ready to offer their arrogant and misconceived predictions about what African families needed.

After decades of such false starts such as this, it became clear to most scientists and doctors that malnutrition was caused simply by a combination of economic and social factors rather than by any of the mistaken, not to say grossly implausible, theories that had obsessed earlier researchers, Western governments and aid agencies. What emerged from this prolonged saga were the flawed and discriminatory beliefs of Western politicians and scientists about Africa and its real needs. Their readiness to jump in with ill-thought-out responses was frequently coupled with an eagerness to offer inappropriate and commercially profitable fixes. This conduct certainly did nothing to deal with malnutrition and, more likely, worsened the problem.

The headline news about Wasting is that there are now successful treatments. These are often based on peanuts, with names such as 'Plumpy Nut', and go under the more generic designation – ready-to-use-therapeutic-foods (RUTF). They are now mass-manufactured, often outside Africa, and widely available in clinics and hospitals. Many children died from being acutely malnourished before such treatments were discovered. Thanks to these high-energy products, the number of deaths from Wasting has significantly reduced in recent years. Yet, other formulations, available under the generic name ReSoMal, have been developed to deal with severe dehydration. What, though, is bad news is that Wasting is not so easily preventable. There are no vaccines or pharmaceutical preparations because it is not a condition caused by bacteria or viruses. However, treatment has been heavily medicalised and commercialised. It rarely involves more sensible, practical, and local responses, such as guaranteed and affordable food prices, safe food stores, improved parent education, adequate sanitation, and clean water supplies. Another frequently neglected protective factor would be for girls to be given even primary education so that they and their families can

African Children in Peril

The 13-year-old Malawian boy on the left is a year older than his English friend (reproduced by permission of Alamy)

be aware of the need for them to be well-nourished before and throughout pregnancy.

Stunting is now the much more widespread but far less well-known form of child malnutrition. Doctors had long been familiar with this chronic condition, which leads to children becoming well below average in height for their age.

However, Stunting did not attract anything like the scientific attention that acute malnutrition had done during the first half of the twentieth century. This was most surprising given the existence of a UK government-funded Medical Research Council research unit in Uganda. It wasn't until the 1980s that stunting received the attention it deserved as the most common form of child malnutrition and the most dangerous in terms of the harm it has caused many children. Although the global number of affected young children is slowly reducing, it still affects over 150 million worldwide. It is a significant causal factor in 45 per cent of children's deaths under five years. It is caused by infants' chronic undernourishment starting from conception and during their vital first two years of life. This period of about 1000 days is when all babies should be developing rapidly and have adequate nutrition to grow normally. This period is crucial when, not only do their bodies grow physically, but when their brains and cognitive abilities should also be developed. It is hard to understand why this condition was not recognised as highly significant until recently. It may be because researchers were so obsessed with ideas about 'tropical diseases' that they failed to see what now appears obvious. Both conditions – Wasting and Stunting – are primarily the result of poverty, inadequate diets and highly adverse environmental conditions such as the lack of clean water or proper sewerage.

Stunting has been described in the South African Early Childhood Review as *'a largely invisible condition that is starving Africa's children's potential'.*[9]

And if, and for whatever reason, children are not fed adequately over these crucial 1000 days, their healthy development is bound to be significantly impaired. It severely damages children's intellectual and emotional development, as shown in their severe lack of school progress and later as college students, workers, and even their competence as parents and citizens. It is very likely too to have lifelong and irreversible consequences for them.

Stunting afflicts over two-fifths of very young children in more than a dozen countries in sub-Saharan Africa and averages more than a third across the region. If the wealthier nations in the northern hemisphere were affected on this scale, there would be overwhelming demands for emergency action. For decades though, the issue was overlooked and given little attention. It was seen as just another manifestation of life in Africa rather than a vital warning sign of a genuinely significant child health problem

Infant mortality rates across sub-Saharan Africa are, on average, 16 times higher than in developed countries. Some important efforts to reduce these frighteningly high stunting levels have now begun, mainly through a recent and highly significant United Nations initiative, 'Scaling up Nutrition'. Already, global incidence rates are starting to decrease, albeit very slowly. But even these welcome changes are offset by higher than expected birth rates in the world's poorest countries, mainly in SSA. Together, these conditions, Wasting and Stunting, directly and indirectly, cause enormous suffering across SSA, with communities and families ravaged by their impact on their children.

There has been a great deal of research investigating the causes of chronic malnutrition. The picture is complicated, and the reasons are many, but they mainly fall into three not immediately apparent categories: food security, maternal care and health resources.

These are somewhat technical terms and, in one sense, perhaps obvious, but they do merit some explanation. They represent the key 'proximal' issues most immediately responsible for malnutrition. There are other so-called 'distal' or background factors, too. These include poverty which is, undoubtedly, the most critical and pervasive underlying cause of malnutrition. However, it's essential to recognise that these causes are not, as was once believed, 'endemic' to Africa. As will become apparent, they are the direct outcome of how Europe has dealt with Africa over many centuries.

Food security

This is probably not a familiar term for most people in the West. Here, it can usually be taken for granted now that, subject to parents being able to afford it, food is always available in shops, and the issue is simply deciding what to buy. For example, many Western supermarkets have aisles of different breakfast cereals. Shoppers are spoiled for choice when purchasing their groceries, especially fruits and vegetables. But in developing countries, things are very different. There is, at best, minimal choice, and there is often no choice about what food is available. Farmers cannot even rely on getting paid for their crops. In recent years in Kenya, farmers have told me that they have repeatedly been refused payment quite arbitrarily by sugar companies. Such unjustified conduct inevitably leaves families without money to buy food.

A major United Nations report[10] on food security in 2015 looked in depth at the causes of food insecurity. It concluded: *'The fundamental right to food – and the right to life itself- is still overlooked in sub-Saharan Africa. Famines and food crises continue to plague the region as nowhere else. The intolerable cycle and hunger, starvation and despair that traps many Africans shows no signs of relinquishing its grip'.* The report makes a crucial point about the vital link between food, food security and human development. It states frankly: *'Famines grab headlines, but chronic food insecurity and malnutrition are the more insidious, often silent, daily calamities for millions of Africans'.* The current war in Ukraine has an enormous impact on food prices in East Africa and on precarious family budgets. In the West, food costs take up to 10% of family incomes, and price increases can be managed to some extent. However, in SSA, the cost of food can exceed 50% of most families' budgets, and any price increase can be an impossible burden.

Maternal care

Again, this term has a very different meaning in developing countries than in the West. With few exceptions, it is generally understood what kind of care and feeding is needed by babies from their mothers. But in the poorest countries, it cannot be assumed that mothers have had any schooling to equip them to be aware of what foods their babies need or that their own health is good enough to care for their babies they might otherwise wish. They are often so poorly fed that they cannot nurture their babies during their pregnancies or breastfeed them.

Health resources

In wealthy countries, parents and children can easily access a general practitioner and a trained midwife. There are always local hospitals where specialist services are available from highly qualified obstetricians and paediatricians in emergencies. They, in turn, can access readily available technical assistance, laboratories and hi-tech equipment such as scanners. The differences in the level of provision are startling. For example, there is one trained doctor in the UK for every 300 people, whereas across SSA, the figure is 1 to 70,000. That means that for every doctor in SSA, the UK has more than 230.

'Health Resources' also refers to the broader health environment where families live, and children grow up. That includes the comprehensive availability of clean running water, decent household sanitation, and proper sewerage. But in sub-Saharan Africa, most of these are unavailable or inaccessible to families, who often live in very rudimentary conditions that pose severe health risks, especially for their young children.

Underlying all these practical problems, families' absolute poverty – having less than $1 per day per person- is an ever-present problem across southern Africa.

In most developing countries, the precarious state of women's health contributes significantly to the numbers of stunted children and, tragically, to very high rates of maternal deaths that are still far higher than in the West. In Niger, for example, a former French colony, the maternal death rate is 90 times greater than in France. In Kenya, formerly a British colony, the mortality rate is 50 times higher than in the UK (WHO Statistics for Health-2018).[11]

No medical or pharmaceutical treatments currently exist to help Stunted children. Several initiatives are being tested to prevent children's chances of stunting in circumstances where this might have been previously unlikely. And other studies are currently being carried out to assess whether it is possible to reduce the impact of the condition that was once thought to be permanent. But these are still unrealised dreams and not the reality of life for most families in sub-Saharan Africa.

Sub-Saharan African countries, together with India and Pakistan, have more than 50 per cent of such cases globally. The number of stunted children is increasing in sub-Saharan Africa's poorer countries because of their higher birth rates. Burundi has a Stunting rate of 58 per cent, and the average figure across the three nations of East Africa (Uganda, Kenya and Tanzania) is above 39 per cent. In Nigeria, the region's most populous country, it is 41 per cent, and in the Democratic Republic of Congo (DRC), its largest, it is 43 per cent. These frightening statistics clearly show the extent of child malnutrition across SSA, not to mention its distressing impact on individual children's health prospects.

The African Early Childhood Review report contains this powerful and most relevant statement about the importance of dealing with child malnutrition in South Africa; *'We will never tackle inequality effectively if we do not support our children's growth and development. There is one injustice, in particular, one potent manifestation of South Africa's persistent poverty and inequality, that exemplifies our failure to unlock human potential and economic growth. That injustice is the astoundingly high levels of nutritional Stunting in South Africa.'*

The fact of it coming from South Africa, the wealthiest country by far in the region but still a very divided and unequal nation, is highly significant. It has been more than 25 years since President Mandela came to power. However, although these years have seen the end of Apartheid without the violence that many predicted, it is sad that present levels of economic inequality in South Africa are among the highest in the world and are matched very closely by racial divisions.

Notes and Guide to Further Reading
'Levels and Trends in Child Malnutrition' UNICEF, World Health Organisation and the World Bank (2020),[12] malnutrition globally.

'Improving Child Malnutrition – The achievable imperative for global progress,' (2013) UNICEF[13] makes for sobering reading. It points out that undernutrition makes young children much more likely to die from treatable conditions such as diarrhoea and pneumonia. It raises the question of why child malnutrition has still not been made history.

'World Health Statistics – Monitoring Health for the SDGs', WHO.[14] This is the most definitive source of global data about every aspect of the United Nations initiative taken to improve the state of world health across all member nations. This has been done to measure achievements towards the realisation of what are called the Sustainable Development Goals, set as targets to be met by 2030. The statistics include relevant figures about child health and nutrition. They describe the position in every member country and also in regional groupings, including sub-Saharan Africa.

'The Riddle of Malnutrition: The Long Arc of Biomedical and Public Health Interventions in Uganda , Tappan.
Here, American sociologist Jennifer Tappan examines how British researchers in Uganda investigated severe child malnutrition during the mid-twentieth century. Her book is an alarming account of the mistakes made by doctors and scientists in attempting to understand and find simplistic treatments for this dangerous condition.

In *'Global Health in Africa'*[15] Tamara Giles – Vernick and James Webb Jr. describe how biomedical practitioners have often failed to appreciate that social science can offer a broader perspective about what has been seen as just 'medical' problems. They rightly warn how dangerous it can be when preconceived technical interventions – such as those to do with malnutrition or family planning – can have long-term and unexpected consequences.

John Iliffe's *'Africans – the history of a Continent'*[16] is a scholarly account, slightly dated now, but has been described as 'superseding all other single volumes of African history. It is grounded in solid research, as might be expected from this distinguished academic. The writing is more nuanced and less personal than in the other books mentioned here. It tells the story of Africa's engagement with the West, right from the emergence of food-growing communities and trade and on to slavery and Colonisation. It ends with a very well-informed account of the Apartheid period in South Africa and a detailed and fascinating description of the international response to the impact of HIV-AIDS on Africa. His concluding and sympathetic remarks about the continent are about *'the notions of honour and family duty'*, which characterises how Africans have dealt with adversity, both in respect of Colonisation and then HIV-AIDS.

However, even this respected historian fails to give much attention to the impact of Western incursions on Africa's children. In his scholarly account of the development of medical schools in East Africa, for example, he is too uncritical about how European training models were thoughtlessly imported, with little regard to how they might meet most citizens' health care needs in a different continent with entirely different histories and social cultures.

Basil Davidson was the first writer to successfully draw the world's attention to the evidence of Africa's ancient and very sophisticated cultural and archaeological history. In *A History of West Africa*[17] he vividly writes about Africa's lost cities and civilisations that had long preceded the slave trade and Europe's cultural and industrial revolutions. No one has done more to describe and make known the rich history of Africa and to make nonsense of the arguments that the continent was a cultural and economic 'blank slate' that legitimised Western incursions and aggressive colonisation. Most other writers have failed to do this and have left an impression that Europeans can claim all the credit for bringing civilisation to Africa when nothing could be further from the truth.

The Neglected crisis of Undernutrition: Evidence for action, DfID 2009[18]. This is a valuable background UK government paper, well worth using as a sound guide to definitions, and statistics, although these are somewhat dated.

Chapter 2

What have been the underlying causes of such widespread disadvantages for children?

What could have brought about the dangerous and enduring poverty levels and the other contributory factors in SSA, which are now known to be the historic and current causes of widespread child malnutrition and deaths? The West's exploitative campaigns and incursions over the centuries in Africa have almost certainly been, as will become apparent, the most critical events that have led to the continuous lack of development of the region and caused enormous damage to families, especially those with very young children.

Before looking at these episodes and judging their impact, it is essential to know what environments children need to grow, learn and flourish. It must be understood that this is true for African children's needs which are no different from those of children everywhere.

All children need:

1. To feel secure and have a stable environment
2. To have loving parenting
3. To have adequate nutrition
4. To have clean water and hygienic surroundings – free from the risk of infection and disease
5. To have access to good health care.

It has long been known that anything that disrupts family environments can cause harm to their children. Some highly respected expert authors such as Brazelton and Greenspan suggest further refinements.[1] Still, the five listed here are the universal litmus tests for judging whether children's needs are being met.

Every social worker knows that families in excessively stressful circumstances can be numbered by thousands, even in modern Britain. Of course, families can be remarkably resilient. Still, if they are subjected to high levels of stress or denied their fundamental human rights, this will inevitably make it very difficult, if not impossible, for parents to protect their children adequately. Current examples of this abound and range from the damaging effect on parenting seen in Afghanistan after the dramatic exit of American forces, to Uganda after two years of Covid lockdown on families whose livelihoods and incomes have been disrupted. In both of these countries, parents have little chance of providing stability, let alone adequate nutrition, for their children. Less dramatic or noticeable circumstances where parental care can be inadequate and children suffer are still to be found daily in the poorer areas of British towns and cities where families live in poverty or insecure housing. The recent setting up and take-up of food banks emphatically demonstrate that family poverty remains a widespread problem even in Britain, the world's sixth most prosperous nation.

The historical episodes in which the West has been involved in Africa have had a far more detrimental impact on families than these present-day examples and have been– as will become clear – grievously harmful to children's healthy growth and development. The most damaging of these various events for Africa, beyond argument, was the Atlantic Slave trade. Even the right-wing historian Niall Ferguson, who in his book, *Empire: How Britain Made the Modern World*[2], glosses over the reality of the British Empire's growth, but does not deny or try to cover up the facts about the levels of brutality and aggression involved in slavery. Another contemporary writer, John Darwin, goes even further in justifying the period of Empire as being of positive benefit to Britain and the rest of the World. However, in *Unfinished Empire*[3] he overlooks the enormous damage that British expansionism caused, especially in Asia and Africa. His unfeeling account of centuries of callous exploitation will comfort many on the right whose forebears benefitted greatly from the proceeds of what amounted to international theft. Not satisfied with this one-sided description, he, like some other writers, tries to justify centuries of British greed by suggesting that this was somehow morally justified by the country's widespread subsequent support for the slave trade to be abolished. This is not true and will be described later. There was extensive and lasting opposition to abolition from many senior politicians and even the British Royal Family.

Slavery was the most destructive event of all, measured by its utterly ruthless brutality over the many decades it was perpetrated by the Western powers. It stole tens of millions of Africans from their homelands and left behind a ravaged, looted, and unstable continent of countless shattered communities and families. It was almost certainly slavery that formed the foundation stone of discrimination and prejudice towards Africans, leading to Africa's subsequent and continued exploitation. Furthermore, it created a legacy of profound and poisonous racism still very apparent today. Slavery would still have left a very long shadow if it had been the only Western incursion to have affected Africa.

But slavery was not to be the only damaging event to impact Africa. Six countries, Britain, France, Portugal, Italy, Spain and Germany, collectively decided on their terms at the end of the 19th Century to take over the continent. This involved a prolonged period of acquisitive and aggressive assaults – Colonisation – by these Western governments. No leaders or citizens of any African countries were ever consulted, let alone involved in these plans. Slavery and Colonisation have had the most damaging consequences for African children. Still, there were other highly significant events, I believe, all set out below, which, together, were the critical contributory causes of the predicament of Africa's children, including widespread malnutrition, ill health, and early deaths. Nothing is definite in history, and there are, no doubt, other factors that some might want to be considered, such as climatic conditions, endemic diseases, corruption and issues of poor governance by African leaders. But only the following events can adequately explain the sheer scale of disadvantage suffered by African children over the centuries.

- The Atlantic Slave Trade and its Impact on Families and Children in Sub-Saharan Africa (seventeenth-nineteenth centuries)
- Colonialism and its Impact on Families and Children in Sub-Saharan Africa (nineteenth-twentieth centuries)
- Neo-Colonialism 'The last stage of Imperialism' (1950s to present)
- Tropical Medicine and its failures to deal with child health and malnutrition and prevent widespread child mortality (nineteenth-twentieth centuries)
- The historical failure by the World Bank to introduce Primary Health Care despite it being recommended by the World Health Organisation (1982-present)
- Neo-Liberalism and Globalisation (1970s-present)

I contend these have been the critically significant events in which Western policies and actions have caused the most harm to the children of SSA. They are chosen from a review of the extensive research and scholarship undertaken by academics and politicians worldwide. They draw particularly from Walter Rodney's seminal study *How Europe underdeveloped Africa*[4], the ideas and extensive writings and speeches of two remarkable African Presidents, Kwame Nkrumah and Julius Nyerere, and the pioneering research about the history of Africa undertaken by Basil Davidson. They also broadly correlate with the more nuanced views and contributions in the *Oxford Handbook of Modern African History*.[5] However, their ideas are primarily about politics, governance, economics and culture. In contrast, my emphases and concerns are entirely about children, mainly their health and nutrition, topics rarely discussed in most academic studies.

The Atlantic Slave Trade was the first and by far the worst of these Western-imposed calamities for African children. It created the springboard for all that followed. Britain officially abolished the Slave trade in 1807, and Slavery was made illegal almost everywhere by the late nineteenth century. Because these dates are so far in the past, it is frequently argued that slavery can no longer be relevant to today's world. But this, and the other related episodes described here, have amounted to the systematic and ongoing neglect by the West of the needs and rights of millions of very young children in the world's poorest nations. Some might argue that this claim is both far-fetched and biased, but how else can the sheer scale of the present plight of children in SSA be otherwise explained? It will also be said that no one planned to cause such widespread harm to children, let alone the very young. Still, unquestionably, enormous and lasting harm has been done, as will become apparent when we examine in more detail the outcome of each of the actions taken by the wealthy countries of the West. Their economic interests were always put before the needs of children in Africa when choices needed to be made. This assertion will be uncomfortable for many. But it is time that the facts about the West's deliberate and continuing exploitation and neglect of Africa and their impact on children are made known and accepted as valid. These have been the causes of the avoidable deaths of many millions of young children in Africa over the past five centuries and extend to the present.

Only by disentangling and analysing these actions separately and carefully will it be possible to examine more precisely how they have impoverished the countries of southern Africa and demonstrate the extent to which the West has been responsible for the harm done to the region's children. Without this evidence, It may not be easy for many to accept that such large-scale damage has directly resulted from Western actions – or to appreciate that it continues today.

Whether in the form of cheap imports of rare minerals or natural products imported on the backs of poorly paid African workers, the West still takes advantage of Africa on a massive scale. It hasn't been easy to uncover the facts about these events in European and British history. Those who have become rich or influential on the proceeds of slavery or colonisation in the past or unfair trade deals today don't want the details of how they or even their forebears have gone about it. It is convenient for Prime Ministers, governments, companies, and individuals to hide behind a raft of untruths and lies that disguise what happened. As the 'Black Lives Matter' campaign gathers momentum, many in power or whose family histories link them to the impoverishment of Africa still try to deny that Britain is racist or cannot accept that what is often taught as 'our history' is often very far from the truth. In his recent book, *Empireland*,[6] the historian and journalist Sethnam Sanghera powerfully demolishes many of the myths still associated with British Imperialism and highlights the readiness of so many people to believe that it was actually beneficial to the colonised countries. The recent British Prime Minister Boris Johnson has said, *'We cannot now try to edit our past. We cannot pretend to have a different history'*.[7]

In the debate about the toppling in Bristol of the statue of the leading slaver Edward Colston and the recent acquittal by a jury of those charged with this offence, British government ministers threatened to tighten legal powers to prevent and punish such citizen action. Other Ministers have repeated this position. The Education Secretary even published guidance for schools restricting open debate about the British Empire. These defensive and highly questionable positions are dangerous in a genuine democracy. They frequently don't stand up to scrutiny by lawyers or historians with access to recent findings from reliable sources, including government archives. The Communities Secretary's decision that all UK public buildings fly the Union Flag seems, for example, like a naïve and superficial attempt to whitewash Imperial history instead of honestly coming to terms with its uncomfortable reality.

A strongly contested report about *Race and Ethnic Disparities*[8] in Britain was recently produced by a Commission set up by the government in the wake of the Black Lives Matter campaign. That report controversially asserted that institutional racism no longer exists in Britain and attempts to offer a different and progressive 'narrative'. It even suggests that slavery allowed enslaved people to learn and 'move on' from their experiences. Many highly respected academics and historians have rebuffed and distanced themselves from these contentious findings and conclusions. Even the UN's special rapporteur for the UK has urged the government to reject the report and warned that *'falsifying historical facts may license further racism and discrimination'*.[9]

It is very concerning that the government should have felt it necessary to go to such lengths to resist any challenges to its particular and cosy view of Britain's history. All histories need to be open to revision in light of new knowledge about past events. It is surprising that a government should want to preserve an incorrect story of Britain's past, and worth examining why this is being done. It looks as if the massive support in the UK for the Black Lives Matter campaign has triggered a panic response. Politicians seemed to fear that if that campaign gathered momentum, there could be threats to the familiar and comforting story of Britain's past and could become a serious destabilising factor if many more people started to understand just how fragile that story is. It is, of course, true that this remarkable and small country did stand alone against Fascism at the beginning of the Second World War, and it was undoubtedly a world power during the era of its global Empire. It is a memorable Churchillian story that allows some contemporary politicians to choose to act as if Britain is still the same leading nation with an unquestioned right to be at the very centre of World affairs, a member of the G7 group of leading countries, and a member of the United Nations Security Council. In fact, the post-Brexit UK and post-Empire is by no means the power it was in the past and now sits alongside several other similar-sized nations, including Germany, France and Italy, in terms of its GDP and the well-being of its citizens.

Such thinking seems inimical to those on the right of British politics and members of the Establishment – whose legitimacy appears to depend significantly on the history of their position and wealth never being seriously questioned. An analysis of how they acquired their privileged positions seems threatening to them. Whether this fear is justified will be examined later, but why the government has been attempting to rewrite British history raises serious questions and underlines how important it is to get to the truth of Britain's historical involvement in racism and colonialism. Britain, like other countries involved in slavery and colonialism, must be honest about its past to be respected worldwide. It cannot hope to deny its history and be credible in current world affairs.

Notes and Guide to Further Reading

Walter Rodney's *How Europe Underdeveloped Africa*, Nairobi: Pambazuka Press, 1972

Written nearly fifty years ago by the Guyanian historian and academic Walter Rodney in this magnificent and still laceratingly critical thesis. Angela Davis describes the book as *'A classic study of the impact of European capitalism on the continent of Africa, which continues to provoke, inspire and educate – it resonates more than ever today.'*

Rodney's study is impossible to dismiss. He critically covers slavery and colonisation before dealing with the post-colonial period as similarly damaging to newly independent African nations. His own story is tragic. He was assassinated in 1980 when only 38 in Guyana as the then president's political opponent during a national election campaign. His book, written when he was just 30, still stands decades later as the definitive history of Europe's one-sided relationship with Africa. His analysis is very penetrating and rigorous, especially as it might have been much more passionate than it was. His intellect and analytical skills shine through in a masterpiece of scholarship and, in Angela Davis's words, *'A landmark in African studies, not to mention the history of colonialism and imperialism. Beautifully written and expertly argued, it is that rare book that can be called a classic – it belongs on every bookshelf.'*

Africa, the roots of revolt Jack Woddis, 1960[10]
These essays were memorable and influential accounts of absolute poverty in Africa and the African case for liberation from colonisation. Jack Woddis was a radical and controversial thinker decades ahead of his time in the USA. He wrote, *'Imperialist rule, far from bringing about progress, led to a catastrophic decline in the standard of living of the African people.'* His words still resonate as frank and uncomfortable testimony to Western greed and exploitation.

Freedom and Unity, Julius K Nyerere 1965[11]
Nyerere was one of Africa's most remarkable and visionary leaders and a man of high principles. He saw the need for African countries to take responsibility for their futures once freed from colonialism and the undue dominance of

the West. As the first President of Tanzania, some of his more radical ideas about communitarianism were unpopular, and he was eventually defeated in national and peaceful elections. He stood down graciously and is remembered as an outstanding, if fallible, politician.

Section 2

The Most Likely Causes

Chapter 3
The legacy of the Atlantic Slave trade for African families and children

What impact, it will be asked, could the Atlantic slave trade possibly have on the current Black Lives Matter (BLM) movement in America and Europe and the health of young children in sub-Saharan Africa today?

BLM has come about primarily as a consequence in the United States of the destructive long-term impact slavery has had on the millions of Africans shipped across the Atlantic. Although very much connected with particular and recent events in America, including the killing of black citizens by the police, it has raised the issue more widely about how people of colour are still being discriminated against in Britain and other parts of the world. It has raised more generally a challenging public conversation about Britain's past involvement in Slavery even though this episode in British history is long past. It has led to much greater public debate and questioning whether institutional racism exists in official bodies such as the police and Home Office in Britain, especially how black immigrants from the Caribbean were treated in the 1960s.

However, the extensive and lasting damage caused by the widespread sacking of the African communities and families left behind has received far less attention. Some historians have naively suggested that the affected communities would have been 'resilient'. This suggestion flies in the face of what is now known about the impact of violent attacks on communities in Europe and the Middle East after wars and civil uprisings. After WW2, much of Europe was a wasteland with millions of displaced peoples suffering from the destruction of their factories, homes and cities.

The point of entering this debate here is not to go over the past as such but, more specifically, to examine the connections between European involvement in Africa and the present-day predicament of so many sick and malnourished African children. Some might question how or even whether these consequences could have resulted from past decades of slavery across many African countries, which involved capturing and enslaving millions of citizens, predominantly men. Their enslavement, though, not only left huge gaps in their families but left their wives and children terrified to move outside their homes or cultivate their gardens and farms. It's not too difficult, on closer examination, to see how much damage – socially and economically – was done to Africa by centuries of rampant slavery. Eric Williams, who was later to become the President of Trinidad and Tobago, has written in *Capitalism and Slavery* the definitive account of this[1]. He describes the broader economic and unstoppable continental momentum associated with slavery, regardless of its directly destructive impact on enslaved African citizens.

The racial prejudice and immiseration of the entire region brought about by slavery were, without a doubt, the fundamental bases for all that was to follow, especially for later generations of children.

It is now universally agreed that children everywhere have an absolute right to be adequately fed, and most of the West's children are now just that. It was not always the case. In the eighteenth and nineteenth centuries, industrial cities, especially in northern Britain, experienced child deaths on a massive scale due to dreadfully poor hygiene and sanitation and inadequate health services. Friedrich Engels[2] described this situation as *Amounting to Murder*. Today, infant mortality rates – more than a hundred years later – are still far higher than average in poor neighbourhoods in Glasgow, Liverpool and East London due to a similar combination of adverse factors, including inequalities of public service provision, poor housing and high unemployment. And during the last decades of the twentieth century, European child malnutrition was rife during the civil war in former Yugoslavia. In parts of the Middle East today, it is still affected by militant Islamism and the internecine struggles between Israel and Palestine. However, unlike a century ago, it is now known that all children must have nourishing food throughout their early years. To do otherwise is sure to cause harm to their proper and healthy development.

Much has been written recently about the killing by police in Minnesota of an unarmed Afro-American man, George Floyd, which has been widely seen as the expression of deeply ingrained prejudice towards black people in the USA dating back to slavery. A similar picture in SSA can be seen in how the West treated every country in sub-Saharan Africa for centuries, starting with slavery. There is a view that slavery is nothing new – that it has long been a part of the world's history – and we are wrong to place so much emphasis on it now. That idea doesn't, however, match the facts. As some right-wing historians assert, it is undoubtedly the case that Africa has long been the target of slavers. From 1400, the slave trade affected Africa for about five hundred years, albeit in four distinct waves; the trans-Saharan, Indian Ocean, Red Sea and the trans-Atlantic slave trades. However, the most significant and deadly of these, when measured by volume and duration, was the Atlantic Slave trade.

The first Western explorers, who were Dutch, made valuable and positive contact with traders from old West Africa from around the fourteenth century. David Olusoga describes this period in *First Contact*[3] very clearly. It is also believed that traders from China had enjoyed similarly civil and respectful contact with Kenyan merchants from as early as the eleventh century. Both the Dutch and Asian visitors had been impressed by the quality of the artefacts and artwork produced by the artisans in inland African kingdoms and were eager to trade with African intermediaries and merchants who were able to sell them tie-dyed fabrics, refined gold and iron, skilfully crafted artefacts as well as ivory. Africans were ready to import cotton, porcelain, and copper goods. This two-way exchange is evidence of how Africa could export dyed cotton goods many years before cotton was grown in Africa and centuries before cotton goods were shipped to Africa from the mills of Lancashire. Portuguese visitors such as the sixteenth-century writer Duarte Barbosa described this period in detail, which admired the so-called 'Swahili' ports of East Africa, including Kilwa and Malindi, *With their tall and handsome houses made of stone and mortar and arranged in streets.*[4] The word 'Swahili' derives, in fact, from the same Arabic word as the Sahel, meaning shore, which in its case meant the shore of an ocean rather than of sand.

The Dutch traders made very similar and admiring comments about West Africa, being the first Europeans to have visited Benin. They described the town as comparable to Haarlem and Amsterdam, with wide streets and fine buildings, all kept immaculately clean and in good order. The people were said to be similar to their Dutch counterparts in their habits of cleanliness and tidiness. When the first Europeans saw the well-built stone buildings at Great Zimbabwe, however, they refused to believe that Africans had constructed them and thought that other white visitors must have been responsible, such was its architectural sophistication.

The more recently understood and well-researched picture of foreigners from both East and West trading with developed and sophisticated African kingdoms runs quite differently than the traditional but inaccurate accounts of Africa being a place of backward peoples who practised cannibalism or worshipped idols. These mistaken beliefs were, though, to become the basis for both Spain and Portugal to feel justified in their slaving expeditions – possibly driven by their antipathy to people who were judged to be different and 'other' and thus not deserving the usual respect accorded, for example, to peoples whose religious beliefs were, for them, more familiar and safe. Before slavery began, the dates varying from West to East Africa, many examples of Africans are recorded of them being treated decently and with respect. One includes a memorable painting in 1650 by the Spanish painter Diego Velasquez of Juan de Pareja, his valued African assistant who became a notable painter in his own right.

Another instance of respectful attitudes towards Africans concerns how King James IV of Scotland welcomed an African woman who landed in a Scottish port in 1506. She was known as 'The Black Lady' and given a highly regarded position within his court, where she was treated with respect and courtesy.

Also significant is the powerful testimony of the renowned Scottish explorer and doctor, Mungo Park, who had travelled alone for more than three years in the late eighteenth century across central Africa, where he had substantial experience of meeting and living with Africans. He wrote, tellingly, in his bestselling and still eminently readable book *Travels in the Interior Districts of Africa:*[5]

> *Whatever difference there is between the negro and European, in the conformation of the nose and the colour of their skin, there is none in the genuine sympathies and characteristic feelings of our common nature.*

In his respected account of poverty in Africa, the historian John Iliffe[6] describes 'poor Africans' condition as very similar to those in preindustrial Europe, with families playing a significant role in alleviating poverty in the absence of institutional support. He considered that levels of malnutrition in Africa were also comparable to those in Britain.

However, none of the examples cited above and at widely differing dates hint at the notion of primitiveness and barbarism that came to be thought of as the prime characteristic of Africa and became the justification for the murderous obscenity of slavery. Where did this come from? It is difficult to find simple reasons why people and nations develop attitudes that permit them to see others as inferior and not worthy of respect. Several explanations have been offered. One highly plausible link between the lack of respect afforded to people of colour and slavery has been suggested. This is about the growth of 'otherness'[7] leading to prejudice. Even today, that process is not easily understood. It seems as if there is an inherent tendency in groups of people to be suspicious of those who are not like them. This may be exaggerated when there is little or no knowledge or experience of the other groups. It might explain why travellers like Mungo Park and the early traders who had become familiar with Africans were much better placed to see them as human beings similar to themselves.

However, and despite that evidence of shared humanity, and just four years after the 'Black Lady' episode in Scotland, the Spanish government issued regulations concerning their intentions to forcibly transport many thousands of Africans like cattle across the Atlantic and into Slavery in the Caribbean. The juxtaposition of these events over such a short time defies easy explanation. Those in powerful positions in Spain and Portugal who had no direct experience of Africans may have simply relied on uninformed, biased and fearful accounts about Africa. It's also probable that the rigid and dogmatic beliefs held by the Catholic Church made it less likely that they would, especially at that time, be open-minded about people who were not like them. (This explanation found expression in the well-known film *The Mission* about the exploitation of Native Americans in South America when Spain and Portugal began colonising another continent.)

Explanations for Britain's first involvement in slavery more probably lie in its strong endorsement by the Royal Family, followed by British merchants' eagerness to find cheap labour sources and markets for their new mass-produced manufactures. One significant version of this idea is termed *Gentry Capitalism*.[8] Certain well-connected international bankers such as the Lascelles, Barings, Lloyds and Barclays saw and took advantage of the broader opportunities that Slavery offered them to make their fortunes.

The Atlantic slave trade was to last for more than twelve generations over four centuries and involved the transportation of more than 20 million Africans. It set the scene for the growth of a harsh 'industry' that has never been rivalled in its cruelty. The facts and terrors of slavery are now well known, and it is not the purpose of this book to repeat them at length. One recently described episode taken from a new account by Nicholas Rogers[9] will suffice to demonstrate the extent of the inhumanity shown by slavers towards African children. It tells how one 15-year-old girl was treated on a slaving ship sailing from Africa to the Caribbean. It concerns Captain Kimber, captain of the slaving ship 'Recovery' based in Bristol, and how he ill-treated this unnamed African girl on his boat. She had tried to hide her modesty after being raped and infected with gonorrhoea. The treatment that was meted out to her was so brutal that she collapsed in convulsions and later died from her injuries. One of his seamen, who had dared to provide evidence against him, was transported for life to Australia. When Kimber's conduct ultimately resulted in him being tried for her murder, he was, unbelievably, acquitted by the Admiralty court judge after a hearing lasting for just 5 hours.

The immensely destructive shift in the relationship between the West and Africa brought about by slavery seems highly likely to have been the foundation of what was to follow in the complete collapse of the respectful Western view of Africans as fellow human beings which had predated slavery.

Elikia M'bokolo has described Atlantic slavery as *Engendering the racism and contempt from which Africans still suffer*.[10] It was also a crucial trigger for the West's subsequent exploitation of the African continent. The supporters of slavery used many arguments to justify their work – eugenics, religion, race, skin colour, Divine Will, intelligence, etc. They were and remain entirely arbitrary distinctions without any scientific foundation.

The most likely explanation of the timing of the beginning of large-scale intercontinental slavery is that it was about the British economy's demands when her territorial ambitions both in Europe and in her Empire were growing. Labour that seemed to be 'free' must have been enormously attractive to businessmen and industrialists in the West, especially if they could argue, as they did, that there were no significant ethical or moral counterarguments to oppose such a trade. The British Royal Family's little-known but very substantial leadership and involvement also played a large part in the growth of the Atlantic slave trade. This started as early as 1571 when Elizabeth 1 gave John Hawkins's slaving expeditions Royal backing. The Royal Family's direct participation began in 1660 when James Stuart, the Duke of York, and the brother of Charles 11, who later took the throne as James 11, gave the Royal Africa Company a monopoly on the slave trade. William Pettigrew provides a comprehensive account of the Company and its link to the Royal Family, as well as to Edward Colston.[11]

The Company was responsible for shipping more than 200,000 slaves to the Americas over the next eighty years, a figure greater than any other organisation in the Atlantic slave trade history. Its first Governor was the Duke of York (DoY), and its deputy Governor was the Bristolian merchant Edward Colston. It transported 6000 enslaved people a year to markets in the Caribbean. They were branded either with the Duke of York's or Company's initials, DoY or RAC, on their chests. In its monopoly, 50 per cent of all the profits made by the RAC went, by decree, to the Crown. Between 1662 and 1731, Over 40,000 of the slaves transported by the Company died en route. Royal support for slavery was later given further and even more emphatic official government endorsement when the English and Spanish governments agreed to jointly promote the growth of slavery through the Treaty of Utrecht of 1713, which gave England the sole rights – or *'Asiento de negroes'* – to transport slaves from Africa to the Spanish colonies of South America and the Caribbean for 30 years. The Royal Family again significantly assisted in this. Queen Anne and John Churchill, the 1st Duke of Marlborough, played a vital part in these discussions. When Queen Anne died childless in 1714, her successor George 1, inherited her shares and went on to buy even more.

Money-making was not confined to the immediate profits from the sale of slaves or the imports of sugar from plantations. It included many other activities linked to the trade: shipbuilding companies, the metalwork industries responsible for making manacles and chains, and the businesses involved in making the barrels and casks needed to ship sugar from the Caribbean. Merchants and bankers in Bristol, Glasgow, London and Liverpool were keen to get involved in what seemed likely to be lucrative work, especially after the Royal Family had so publicly approved it. Other companies included the textile manufacturers interested in making the clothes required by sailors, overseers and slaves on plantations. Slavery-related commercial activity in these ports and their surrounding towns and regions was the key to the significant expansion of British business. Many 'decent citizens' in Britain and other European countries saw no objections to Slavery and, at its height, over 40,000 British citizens, including clergymen and government ministers, were unapologetically involved, directly and indirectly, in the ownership of slaves and the Caribbean sugar plantations where most were forced to work. They referred to the 'sugar trade' rather than admitting to being involved with the brutality of Slavery in which human lives meant nothing.

Foremost amongst those who supported and helped finance slavery was Edwin Lascelles, later Earl Harewood, who built Harewood House near

Leeds. Lascelles owned more than 20 plantations and more than 2000 slaves, becoming one of the wealthiest slave owners in the Caribbean with funds made too from other deals, some highly questionable, to supply goods and services to other slavers. In the late eighteenth century, Henry Lascelles became the Collector of Customs for the port of Bridgetown in Barbados. He and, later, his brother Edwin may also have defrauded other slavers and merchants for several decades due to being in that important position. The family has had financial and property interests in the Caribbean for over 300 years, up to as recently as 1975. Their present eminence as a family with direct and recent Royal connections owes everything to their joint and extensive involvement with the slave trade.

Today, Harewood House, a popular 'tourist destination', stands in its hundreds of acres as a monument to the enormous fortunes that its original owner and company accumulated right at the centre of the slave trade.

There was little mention of its dubious history in a recent Harewood leaflet about its origins, euphemistically described as part of 'the sugar trade'. Its fabulous art gallery, full of expensive paintings and sculptures, bears witness to the prodigious profits which accrued from the pitiless treatments meted out to thousands of enslaved Africans – who were often worked literally to death and where rape was an integral feature of how women were forced into sex with

Harewood House near Leeds

plantation overseers, deliberately to bear children who would become slaves themselves often after being cruelly separated as infants from their mothers.

It is understandable that the present owners of Harewood House, themselves the direct descendants of Edwin Lascelles, want to move on from these connections with Slavery which provided the entirety of the funds required to build such an imposing house and estate. It must be emphasised that they bear no responsibility for past events.

The resistance to acknowledge the past is still to be reckoned with in Britain. The Master of Jesus College in Cambridge has recently been prevented from moving a plaque to Tobias Rustat, a notorious slaver, to a less conspicuous place. Almost unbelievably, the local Church of England diocese has obstructed her reasonable request.

Some others, such as the Codringtons, whose forbears were similarly involved in slavery, are now more open about their history and have acknowledged what their forebears did more frankly. To their credit, the National Trust and English Heritage, bastions of middle-class values in Britain, have undertaken meticulous studies about their properties across the UK, where the income their owners derived from Slavery played any part in their construction.

In the Netherlands, the Dutch national art museum, the Rijksmuseum, plans to open its first major exhibition about Dutch involvement with Slavery. It also plans to respond to restitution claims to return up to 100,000 pieces of art looted from former colonial lands. This initiative may be a reaction to the Dutch prime minister's recent refusal, Mark Rutte, to apologise for his country's past involvement in the slave trade – saying that he thought that to do that would be 'too polarising'.

Some remorse might even be seen in Belgium when. In March 2021, on the sixtieth anniversary of the independence of the DRC, King Philippe of Belgium wrote to the President of the DRC, Felix Tshisekedi. He expressed *'deep regrets for Belgium's previous abuses and the deaths these had caused.'*[12.] Although this falls short of reparations or even a full apology, it is significant because of the earlier remarks of his brother, Prince Laurent, who shamefully defended King Leopold's conduct. He stated that Leopold couldn't be held responsible for what others had done in his name as he had never set foot in the country.

Another example of how some cities are starting to face up to their histories can be seen in the way that Liverpool has recently been more open about its extremely dubious history, which was right at the heart of everything to do with slavery, and ranged from banking to trading and boat building to help slavers during the American Civil War, to its direct and substantial involvement with the actual transport of slaves from Africa to the Caribbean for many decades. Its History of Slavery museum doesn't hold back in its vivid account of the city's role in slavery. Whether this is enough is still an open question, but at least the city hasn't tried to downplay its past involvement. But whether it has learned anything from that history is another question altogether. It was very much involved in race riots in some of its more impoverished areas in the1960s due to blatant discrimination and hostility towards its newly settled Afro-Caribbean citizens.

Other cities substantially involved in slavery, such as Bristol and Glasgow, have not been as open, as evidenced by the recent furore in Bristol about a statue of one of its leading citizens and the most notorious slave trader of all, Edward Matthew Colston. Although the statue has been taken down and placed in one of the city's museums, it was a source of divided opinion in Bristol for centuries. Some still admire his place in history, and others are outraged by what he did. His fortune and many of the city's handsome buildings directly resulted from the slave trade.

Glasgow, too, continues to distance itself from its businessmen's profits only because of their sugar warehouses' positioning several miles away from the city centre. However, the names of many of its streets tell the true story. In Edinburgh, there has been a long-standing controversy about another prominent statue in the city's centre, erected out of respect to one of its politicians, Henry Dundas. At the time of the long-lasting debate about abolishing the slave trade at the end of the eighteenth century, he had been the British Home Secretary. Later, to become the first Viscount Melville, Dundas argued that the 1807 legislation to make the Transatlantic slave trade illegal should be 'gradual', which it was for over a decade. It is argued that more than 500,000 Africans were transported to the Caribbean due to this delay.[13] The controversy about his role in the process of abolition has been fierce. His direct descendants argue that he was not a supporter of slavery. However, Melanie Newton, a Professor of African studies at Toronto University and herself of African descent, describes him as *An out and out supporter of the slave trade and a white supremacist.*[14]

Edinburgh Council, to its credit, has now decided to place a new plaque close to his monument, putting the facts about his role in delaying abolition in public view. This action, reflecting the conflict of opinions between Dundas's direct descendants and those who question his position, may serve as a model of how the story of those involved in slavery can best be told.

During the eighteenth century, when Slave trading was at its peak, many influential voices were raised against it, albeit without success; such were the attractions of the vast fortunes that were to be made, not only by leading bankers and businessmen like Lascelles, Drax, Codrington and Beckford but by many others all too willing to be involved in the Atlantic slave trade to finance the British economy and the growth of its cities and Empire. Since the Black Lives Matter campaign, several other organisations, ranging from some leading UK universities, including both Oxford and Cambridge, who had benefited materially from questionable legacies and the British Library and the Church of England, have been examining their positions and are starting to acknowledge their historical connections to slavery. Some of this seems to be somewhat superficial. Still, it represents some progress, especially in contrast to arch deniers such as the British Museum, which is still robustly, but disgracefully defending its questionable ownership of many treasures and culturally significant artefacts stolen from Africa.

Slavery, in the seventeenth and eighteenth centuries, was not some hole-in-the-corner activity in which a few dubious merchants were active. On the contrary, it was a very substantial, if shabby, part of Britain's past, involving the Royal Family and robustly led by it. Their extensive involvement and support sent a critical signal to the many thousands of citizens who subsequently felt able, without troubling their conscience, to enslave people or become involved in the business of slavery. In a recent and influential study, 'The Interest', the author, Michael Taylor,[15] details the British Establishment's resistance to anti-slavery legislation. It exposes just how embedded slavery had become in Britain as an activity that made fortunes and underpinned the British economy and Britain's place in the world. The popular and comforting myth is that Britain enthusiastically led the way in its principled opposition to slavery and was the first country to legislate to bring a complete end to slavery. This is not true. The first country to outlaw slavery in its entirety was Haiti which did so immediately upon its independence from France in 1804.

In fact, as Taylor meticulously demonstrates, there was widespread resistance during a prolonged process towards the final legislation in Britain, with politicians, including Canning, Peel and Gladstone, not to mention the Duke of Wellington and even King Wiliam IV, all siding with the plantation owners to oppose it.

British legislation finally banning slave ownership was eventually enacted in 1833, followed in 1837 by a further Act giving compensation payments for the slavers but none for the enslaved. The level of compensation was so considerable that those who had been at the heart of slavery, such as the Lascelles and Drax families, became rich beyond belief. These families seem to have remained so, judging by the extravagant buildings and priceless artefacts prominent at Harewood and in Dorset. The sitting Conservative Member of Parliament, Richard Grosvenor Plunkett-Ernle-Erle-Drax, still owns a very extensive estate in Dorset, built from his family's ownership of sugar plantations in Barbados. More than 30,000 slaves died from the brutal treatment meted out to them on the Drax plantations for over 200 years.

The Africanist scholar Patrick Manning[16] describes the destructive impact Slavery had on precolonial African societies. Earlier, some historians such as Phillip Curtin[17] argued, somewhat unconvincingly, that African communities themselves would be resilient, especially after the slave trade ended. A more recent analysis of detailed shipping records by Phillip Lovejoy has thoroughly disproved this view.[18] No less a person than David Livingstone also confirmed the facts of Africa's devastation by the slave trade.[19] He records in his diary and details the widespread damage that Slavery had had on villages, especially those that had lost numbers of their menfolk to slavers. He saw slaves killed by their captors when they were too weak to walk. He describes witnessing a slaver killing a baby by dashing the baby against a tree. He also gives graphic examples of African villagers who, despite having excellent skills as farmers and agriculturalists, were so terrified of the slave hunters that they were scared to leave their villages to work on their plots and could not find adequate food for themselves and their children. As a result, many of them and their children perished·

Due to enslavement, primarily of men, Africa's population declined significantly, and the gender balance became distorted. Guiseppe Bertocchi's[20] recent research on the legacies of slavery in and out of Africa concludes:

> In 1850, Africa had a population of about 50 million. It is estimated that without the impact of slavery, it would have reached about 100 million. Thus, over 250 years, the continent lost half its population.

As well as significantly reducing the size of the population, the ravages associated with slavery must have been extraordinarily disruptive and frightening for the families and children left in Africa. This period must also have been enormously damaging for children's health and nutrition. Comparisons with the terrifying impact on children affected by civil strife in the present day in, for example, Afghanistan or Myanmar seem legitimate. So invasive was the slavery by Arab and African traders that its effects persisted into Africa's economic, political, demographic, cultural, social, and religious life for many centuries. The journal 'New African' has described the impact of slavery in these terms: *Slavery outdistanced in scale and scope any other disasters – natural or manufactured, which have ever descended upon the continent* (M'Baye, 2006).[21]

Many recent and convenient stories about Britain's past Empire building in Africa are self-serving myths. The familiar and comfortable accounts of British 'civilising' colonial history, praised by Boris Johnson and some compliant historians, are just fig leaves to cover up appalling cruelties and criminal behaviour. One distinguished and otherwise respected Oxford scholar who got his facts completely wrong was the Regius Professor of History, Hugh Trevor Roper. He, astonishingly, characterised African history as *The study of 'the unrewarding gyrations of barbarous tribes in picturesque but irrelevant corners of the globe.'*[22]

He is not the first to refuse to recognise that the facts about Empire and Africa differ from what they might wish to believe.

A substantial body of research, such as that by historian Basil Davidson[23] confirms that many parts of pre-colonial Africa had sophisticated and impressive civilisations many centuries before contact with the first European explorers. With more details about that and British and European involvement in Africa still coming to light, politicians who try to deny the facts will be proven wrong. Not surprisingly, much attention has been given to the murderous and sickening harm slavery had on its direct victims. Male slaves were often castrated, and female slaves were sexually abused by overseers and treated as breed stock to produce children who would become labourers on plantations. They could be maimed, murdered or raped at the whim of their owners because they were treated simply as chattels. Their owners frequently sacrificed others at funerals or for religious purposes.

But it is now clear that although slavery's impact was murderously destructive to those enslaved during the centuries of its active existence, its effects on the African families and children who were left behind were also long-lasting and destructive. The most significant long-term harm that slavery had on Africa itself was the legacy of racist prejudice that it left and which still prevails today in how Africa and people of colour are treated. When a group of people were ill-treated in the brutal way that Africans were, without any consequences for their oppressors, it is not surprising that those responsible became accustomed to and insensitive to the harm they had caused. Perhaps there is a parallel between Jewish people's experience in Europe over many centuries and the levels of prejudice, humiliation, and violence that they suffered as a community, eventually leading to the casual violence and murders that characterised Germany's conduct towards Jews during the Second World War.

The disregard and contempt for Africans, which was a defining feature of slavery, has been, almost certainly, the underlying cause of the levels and viciousness of prejudice that exist today in the West. During the long era of slavery, enslaved people were not seen as fellow human beings or worthy of any respect. What other reasons could explain the plight of Black Americans for so long, even extending to their children's rights to education? Why was Martin Luther King, their non-violent leader, assassinated, and why are American police so manifestly hostile to black citizens? What else can explain how the British government is still dealing so cruelly with its Black citizens and children who have settled here decades earlier after being recruited from the Caribbean to work in Britain in the 1970s? This analysis of the long-term impact of slavery and colonialism by the West echoes Jean-Paul Sartre's views when writing about the colonial war in Algeria. He talks about *The 'processes of history… being brought into the clear light of day.*

Such levels of racism and prejudice, essentially engendered by slavery, were also the principal causes of the West's continuing neglect and lack of concern about children's health and well-being so visible today in Africa. The long-term impact of slavery on African children can be seen in three ways.

Firstly, through its direct impact on enslaved people. Between 1550 and 1850, more than 12 million Africans, mainly men, were forcibly transported from the coasts of West Africa and across the Atlantic Ocean. Three million to four million African slaves were shipped to the Caribbean during the nineteenth century alone, and many others died or drowned during these voyages. The obscene barbarity of enslavement itself triggered the appalling way transhipped Africans were then subsequently treated on their arrival in the United States and other receiving countries. This well-documented era must, beyond question, have been the basis for the prejudice and the endemic discrimination shown towards people of colour, both adults and children, which has persisted so clearly, well beyond the end of slavery. That brutalising link has been revealed so clearly by the Black Lives Matter movement in the USA.

Secondly, the subsequent impact of slavery on the communities who remained in Africa after the end of slavery was socially and economically destructive to them and their children. It is thought that the population of those parts of Africa which had been prey to slavers was reduced by more than fifty per cent. This was due to a combination of the loss to slavery of so many economically active citizens and the terrifying and widespread fear of enslavement, which affected agriculture and child nutrition, as well as reproduction rates.

And thirdly, as a consequence of the poisonous and continuous effect that slavery generated on attitudes and racial bigotry toward black African citizens. The slave trade dates from the first contact between Africans and the West more than 600 years ago. The evidence points to a gradual process involving a slow growth of prejudice, which developed into blatant and widespread racism. Both have diminished the respect and regard that the West, both in America and Europe, has had for Africans and which, over time, has fuelled the growth of entrenched and irrational racial prejudice towards African nations and children. This, coupled with the effect of colonialism, more later, seems most likely to have been why the present and high rates of malnutrition and child deaths in sub-Saharan Africa have attracted so little interest and sympathy from the West. Over the centuries, the enormous numbers of infant deaths in the region have counted for nothing because the children were African and black. Their lives were seen as being of little consequence compared to the outrage that would have arisen if they had been white children anywhere in Europe and America.

Notes and brief Guide to Reading
Slavery, Family and Gentry Capitalism in the British Atlantic (2006) S. D Smith
This comprehensive and sobering account describes the Lascelles family's pivotal part in financing and facilitating the British slave trade from 1648 to 1833. No other family had such an involvement in the growth of slavery in the Caribbean and the complex trading network it facilitated between Africa, the Caribbean, North America and Britain. They were right at the centre of this hugely profitable business. They continued to stay involved in the sugar

trade in the Caribbean until 1975, many decades after slavery had been made illegal.

The author concludes his account of this family's involvement with slavery in these telling words;

> *The significance of the Lascelles' lies in the present as much as the past. At Harewood House and many other heritage sites, conversations are beginning to take place about slavery; scenes from history, long obscured, are at last becoming visible.*

Transformations in Slavery; a History of Slavery in Africa (2012)
Paul E. Lovejoy[25]
This immaculately researched study looks in more detail than other histories about how slavery affected Africa, as distinct from how slavers treated slaves. Lovejoy concludes his book with this assertion;

> *We have to increase the level of awareness among scholars, and indeed the public at large, about the experiences of the enslaved throughout history. We have to close the gap in knowledge dissemination to restore the dignity of peoples who have suffered the experience and legacy of slavery.'*

This last phrase is of enormous importance today, as politicians try to impose inaccurate and tendentious views about British history and ignore the experience of millions of families and children in Africa who are still visibly affected by the after-effects of slavery.

Capitalism and Slavery (1943) Eric Williams
This is the classic account of how European capital funded the Atlantic Slave Trade in the seventeenth and eighteenth centuries, viewing it as just another opportunity for bankers and merchants to enrich themselves and which, it was argued, *'would form the basis of Great Britain's naval and imperial supremacy.'*

The author, who became the first Prime Minister of Trinidad and Tobago, explains just how vital slavery was for the British economy and how its profits helped finance the British economy's growth to a point when the worldwide exports from its factories made its dependence on slavery unnecessary. He makes the point, just as relevant today, that slavery should not be seen as some forgettable and forgivable episode in Britain's history but that it must be viewed as a critical underlying driver in the British economy's growth right up to the present time. To deny this, he argues, is to ignore the pain and misery that Britain's past Monarchs, national governments, merchants and bankers imposed upon the peoples of Africa. They carry the responsibility for setting in train the era of slavery that lies behind the dreadful predicament of children still visible across sub-Saharan Africa.

Chapter 4

Colonialism and its damaging social and economic impact on African families and children

The impact of slavery, still today, on Africans and their children's lives cannot be overstated. Slavery set the scene for what to follow in how the wealthy countries of the West felt able, subsequently, to colonise and plunder the subcontinent for its natural and mineral resources and, in so doing, to overlook the needs of African families and their children altogether. The process of superiority, entitlement and demeaning racism that Slavery engendered continued long after it was made illegal. In the USA, too, this has been a conspicuous and shameful feature of life up to the present day and was, it appears, so central to the recent killing by police of George Floyd. In Britain, the widespread involvement with slavery that had permeated so much of British business left a continuing legacy of poisonous prejudice towards Africa and its peoples.

For example, at the 1861 meeting of the London Ethnographical Society – later to become the Royal Geographical Society – and decades after slavery was made illegal, the speaker was the distinguished French traveller Paul du Chaillu. He had recently returned from his journey through the unexplored forests of equatorial Africa. But instead of describing, as many in his audience might have expected, the primitivism and even barbarism of the native Africans he had met on his journey, M du Chaillu surprised them by suggesting that: *'the natives were other than they seemed, and that they possessed certain redeeming features including having a well-established religion.'*[1] Members of that Society were so disturbed by these challenging revelations about peoples whom they had previously called 'leather-skinned Hottentots' that they decided to commission another expedition to Africa led by the better-known traveller and explorer, Richard Burton, whose judgements about Africans could, they felt, could be better trusted. His openly racist and derogatory view of native Africans, of which they would have been aware, was summarised in these utterly racist words: '*Once an African becomes an adult, his mental development is arrested, and thenceforth he grows backwards instead of forwards.*'[2] He didn't disappoint his sponsors. Although he and his companion John Hanning Speke undoubtedly suffered in their journey to the Great Lakes region in central Africa in search for the source of the Nile, his lack of empathy with his African porters, as crudely expressed in his diaries, is almost palpable. Burton didn't see them as fellow human beings but only as beasts of burden, routinely required to carry enormous loads. After this next expedition, he failed to share any significant insights or empathy with Africans' lives and beliefs. But this didn't prevent him from expressing his openly racist opinions, confirming his essential character as an outrageous and boastful egotist. For many people, even now, Sir Richard Francis Burton KCMG, FRGS, was a great explorer and colonialist. But his egotistical motto runs; '*Do what thy manhood bids thee do, from none but self-expect applause*'[3] made it unlikely that he was ever a decent human being, let alone a hero. It's clear from his writings and those of his biographer, Mary Lovell,[2] that this bizarre notion of 'manhood' served as his guiding and shabby principle in all he did. Still, even this hasn't prevented him from being lionised by some as one of the greatest English explorers. One reason is that he gave the eminent fellows of the Royal Geographical Society just what they wanted – a fundamentally prejudiced and racist view of Africa – and, in return, this out-and-out racist was granted their supreme award, the Founders Gold Medal.

Such racism was not confined to explorers such as Burton. It was common in the latter part of the nineteenth century for Africans to be seen not as fellow human beings but as '*other creatures*' and thus not deserve any respect. It has even been suggested that belief in the superiority of Western nations and white men lay in the findings of Charles Darwin, whose seminal study – '*The descent of man by means of natural selection or, the preservation of favoured races in the struggle for life*',[3] raised the issues of race. If superficially and wrongly, this was interpreted as giving others some scientific licence to decide which groups were inferior and thus entitled to impose their cultures and interests on other nations and groups of people. Darwin was neither a eugenicist nor a racist, but as his research and writings did not have access to more modern scientific insights about genetics, it is not difficult to see comparisons between what he wrote and what people like Lord Lever and Cecil Rhodes, both of whom wrote and conveniently believed, that the superiority of the Western nations and their '*God-given right and duty*' to take over other countries, permitted them to disregard their views completely and to profit from that opportunity.

A more recent source of that discrimination and disparagement of Africans lies in how Joseph Conrad chose to describe Congo, the setting of his book about slavery, *Heart of Darkness*, published in 1899, almost a century after slave trading had been made illegal. In unambiguously discriminatory terms, Conrad writes about a voyage on the Congo river:

> *We were wanderers on a prehistoric earth, on the earth that wore the aspect of an unknown planet. We could have fancied ourselves the first of men taking possession of an accursed inheritance.*[4]

His experience of Congo had been limited to a single river journey up the Congo river. Still, he chose to elaborate on that experience by painting a graphic picture of African primitivism and cruelty. This language amply confirms that he didn't believe in shared humanity between the Western travellers and African people, especially when he writes:

> *No, they were not inhuman. Well, you know that was the worst of it – this suspicion of their not being inhuman.*

His description of an atmosphere of murderous dread minimised what was happening in Congo, in that the villain of the piece, Kurtz, was a white racist. For many, Conrad's book has served to justify the unforgivable atrocities being played out in real life by the murderously violent Belgian colonialists in Congo. These grave misgivings about Conrad are given very authoritative support by Chinua Achebe,[5] who is laceratingly critical of him. He quotes this description by Conrad of an African who has received the rudiments of education:

> *And between whiles, I had to look after the savage who was the fireman. He was an improved specimen: he could fire up a vertical boiler. He was there below me and, upon my word, to look at him was as edifying as seeing a dog in a parody of breeches and feather hat walking on his hind legs. A few months of training had done for that fine chap. He squinted at the steam-gauge and the water-gauge with an evident effort of intrepidity – he had filed teeth too, the poor devil and the wool of his pate shaved into queer patterns, and three ornamental scars on each of his cheeks. He*

ought to have been on the bank clapping his hands and stamping his feet on the bank, instead of which he hews hard at work, in thrall to strange witchcraft, full of improving knowledge.

Although these were merely words in a novel, they helped fuel the picture of primitivism in Africa that was so pervasive in Europe during the late nineteenth and for much of the twentieth centuries. Given that the writer was so eminent and respected as Conrad, it's easy to see how many Europeans might have gained a prejudiced and inaccurate view of Africa from his book.

In a British context, evidence of similarly prejudiced views about Africans can be seen in the way that Africans were viewed in Bradford, the Yorkshire mill town, itself built on cheap and often immigrant labour by its wealthy and self-righteous factory owners in the late nineteenth century, later to be ridiculed by T S Eliot in his poem, 'The Wasteland', as *Silk-Hatted Millionaires*. Their lack of interest in matters other than making money was also criticised by the Victorian John Ruskin, who drew attention to the gulf between the city's wealthy men's cultural and pretentious aspirations and the modest reality of their achievements. Even today, their overweening self-importance can be seen in the city's spectacular Undercliffe Cemetery, where their massive marble cenotaphs and winged seraphim must compare in ridiculous ambition with the funeral architecture of any other public cemetery in Britain.

Bradford is my birthplace. As a child, my parents often took me to its most famous park, Lister Park. It was here where a group of bewildered African people, described as 'Hottentots', had, before my time, been kept like animals for the public to view. A sign, now inexplicably missing, told that they lived in the park until their deaths from influenza. So it is not without irony that this same park is now an award-winning showcase site because of its significance in modern-day multi-racial Bradford. It was donated to that city by one of its many self-made millionaire industrialists, Samuel Lister, later to become 1st Baron Masham.

Similar and openly racist exhibitions of native peoples, such as those in touring fairgrounds where they were often described as 'savage cannibal pygmies of the Dark Continent', were not unusual in Victorian England. In another example, drawn again from Bradford, a group of Somalis 'living in their village' was offered as the highlight of the 1904 City of Bradford Exhibition and other displays, mainly about that immensely wealthy city's past industrial success. Their lives were supposedly illustrated each day by demonstrations of dancing, arrow shooting and spear throwing. The Prince and Princess of Wales, later to become King George V and Queen Mary, were guests at the exhibition attended by over 2 million people. It is difficult to believe that this display's purpose was anything other than to allow people to stare at these black strangers and feel superior to them as strangers from a distant continent.

These events were not confined to Britain, and so-called Human Zoos or Ethnographic museums were organised across the USA and, even more ominously, in Germany, up to 1931. In the USA, P.T Barnum organised public human exhibitions from the early years of the eighteenth century. Maximo and Bartola, two microcephalic children from El Salvador, were exhibited in freak shows across the USA and Europe, and exhibitions of exotic peoples were organised in New York and other cities. In 1896 the Cincinnati Zoo ran a display of a hundred invited Sioux Native Americans for over three months. The renowned Sioux leader, Geronimo, was shamefully recorded as being pressed into giving autographs to the visitors. Shortly after the Bronx Zoo opened in 1899, Pygmies from Africa and New Guinea were, it is hard to believe, displayed in the Zoo's Primate section. These and similar events were not just part of a freak show mentality. They were manifestations of a White supremacist/racist school of thought, most egregiously illustrated by a display at the World Fair in St Louis, Missouri, in 1904, where some of the Philippine native people were brought to the USA after the 1898 Spanish-American War when the USA won possession of the Philippines. An event entitled 'A parade of evolutionary progress' was arranged to demonstrate the difference between the American people's superior condition and some of their former adversaries' perceived primitiveness. These events, and many like them, were all intended to demonstrate the backwardness of native peoples and emphasise the West's 'civilising' influence. Far from an isolated illustration of racial prejudice associated with slavery, this illustrates how widespread negative attitudes towards Africa and its peoples were formed and strengthened. They were not accidental events. They took place because it suited the powerful and wealthy elites that ran countries and governments in Europe (and the USA) before 1900, deliberately to see Africa as a benighted continent peopled by primitive and simple natives who, because of their 'otherness', could be exploited. Their resources could be commandeered or stolen at will, without any legal or ethical consequences.

Although it is still not well known, many parts of Africa and the Middle East, and well before the first visitors from outside, enjoyed standards of art, culture and craftsmanship more advanced than in much of Europe. Far from being 'primitive and barbaric', many African regions had rich histories that matched and often surpassed Europe's in terms of arts, commerce, architecture, and artisanal skills, many centuries before any comparable development took place in Europe. Ethiopia, the Nile Valley, Egypt and Sudan were the best known of these African civilisations. These ancient and sophisticated civilisations have long been admired. Many other parts of the continent were also marked by advanced cultures existing over centuries. There were similarly advanced settlements in South and West Africa – in present-day Zimbabwe, Ghana, Mali and Niger – where impressive systems of government and commerce operated and, in the case of West Africa, where valuable metals, especially gold and copper, were mined, refined and crafted into products that were sold as highly desirable and high-quality ornaments and artefacts. Many such items are now displayed and more often just stored in the British Museum as examples of West Africa's brilliant skills and artistic genius, anticipating by many centuries some of the ideas that became the stuff of 'modern art' in the twentieth century. In 1897, following a military setback, British troops stole hundreds of impressive bronze artefacts from Benin in Nigeria. These have ended up in various Western museums, churches and Universities and are the subject of much controversy about whether they should be repatriated to their country of origin. Some curators of these beautiful objects have been keen to return them. In contrast, others, including the British Museum, question whether such treasures should be repatriated or even argue that Nigeria cannot guarantee their safe care. Such debates sit uncomfortably alongside the facts about the original theft of these pieces and the existence of a Nigerian Legacy Trust, set up precisely to provide a secure home for any returned items.

Ethiopia stands out in Africa in its dazzling architectural achievements, rich artistic culture and religious traditions that date back well before Christ and have continued until today. This history places it ahead of most European countries and stands in comparison with the other internationally recognised learning centres in the Middle East. Significantly and unlike elsewhere in Africa, it has never been colonised. This might explain how it has addressed child malnutrition more successfully than other countries, despite its poverty and the damage caused by foreign incursion in the 1930s, civil war and even the more recent dictatorship of the Mengistu era.

Many of Antwerp's present and most spectacular public buildings, including the Royal Museum, were constructed from King Leopold's enormous profits from his rubber plantations. An even more spectacular display of nearly two million artefacts from Congo is still displayed in the Royal Museum for Central Africa, built for the International Exposition of 1897 in Brussels, despite much recent public disapprobation about the history of Belgium's colonisation of Congo. The museum has additional notoriety in that it housed a Congolese village during that exhibition, and seven of the Congolese people involved in this racist display died.

Western views of African history are now changing. Many modern scholars and researchers recognise the weight of evidence that confirms that Africans were just as sophisticated and 'developed' in their communities, cultures and skills as the citizens of the European countries who were to become their colonisers. Of course, Africans did not have the Western technologies which enabled the development of railways, industries, telegraphy, or the deadly armaments made in Europe in the eighteenth and nineteenth centuries. However, there are many examples still being revealed of highly skilled peoples across the continent, architecturally sophisticated buildings, complex and significant townships, government, and trade, as well as an understanding and use of mathematics and science, well before the arrival of the first European travellers.

Basil Davidson's extensive writings have illustrated how Africa had anticipated what was to follow in Europe and the Middle East for many centuries. Many other respected writers and historians have also described how advanced Africa's civilisations and social structures were in the pre-colonial era. They have shown just how rich and proud a history Africa possesses – from well-governed kingdoms and impressive public buildings to regional markets and long-distance trading systems, complex systems of law and government, and many highly skilled artisans working with silk, cotton, and precious metals, as well as highly competent sculptors and architects and, not least important in this analysis, evidence of an appreciation of the importance of hygiene and cleanliness many centuries before these were recognised as such elsewhere.

As one example of the global influence of early African industry, it has been argued that In the city-states of Florence, Genoa and Venice, it was West African gold, the result of the efforts of Africa's miners, merchants and entrepreneurs, that made it possible for the development of capitalism and the growth of prosperity in late medieval Europe. This influence could well be thought to go much further than the use of gold. It could include the much greater number of arts and skills that were commonplace in many parts of

Africa hundreds of years before they reached Europe and have merited much more respect than was given to the continent of Africa than it received from the West.

Another overlooked, but less well-known instance of much earlier African history is at Isimila in Tanzania's Southern Highlands. A most extensive collection of iron age tools dating from 100,000 to 50,000 years ago can be seen in a gully over several hundred metres, unremarked and virtually unprotected. If such an important early site had existed in Britain or any other European country, it would have become a protected World Heritage archaeological site if not part of a national museum celebrating and marking its early history. Researchers have now recognised its importance as a site of very great importance in the development of homo sapiens. However, it wasn't seen by the UK as having any particular significance in the colonial era before Tanzania's independence in 1963, another example, perhaps, of how the British colonial power chose to disregard or even disbelieve the facts of African history and achievements.

During the hundreds of years in which Slavery was rampant, prejudice and murderous racism towards the native peoples of SSA went unchallenged. It was accepted throughout Europe and Britain as somehow 'normal'. Despite the moral outrages which were eventually expressed about slavery, governments and many so-called 'decent citizens' in the late nineteenth century and after the end of slavery as such, went on to think that it was perfectly acceptable and even morally justified to aggressively colonise the poorer countries of the Southern hemisphere in order, and, as it was frequently described: *To bring them the benefits of Christianity, Trade and Civilisation.*[6]

This was done without either the agreement or participation of any African leaders but by using overwhelming and deadly force, particularly during the latter decades of the nineteenth century in what became known as the 'Scramble for Africa', a process of Imperial Colonisation, which today appears to many people now as both shocking in its very concept, and remorselessly brutal in how it was done. Britain and other Western nations saw it as entirely justifiable to invade Africa and pillage its resources and peoples without regard for the terrible harm done to generations of innocent children. Europeans talked as if Africa hadn't existed before it was 'discovered' by them. In a parliamentary debate about colonialism, Lord Salisbury, when British prime minister, even talked about: *British soldiers marching through Africa – where no man had trod before.*

Together, these events contributed to a mindset in which Africans were not seen as human beings, and their invaders openly stated that they didn't even have souls.

The multi-stage process, extending over centuries, going from prejudice to slavery and racism, and eventually to colonisation, has, I suggest, been a critical part of the neglect of child health and nutrition that the global South still faces today. Britain and Europe could hardly have made it more explicit, through their high-handed, not to say brutal, treatment of sub-Saharan Africa, that African children's well-being was of no concern whatsoever. Some of the earlier stages in this process are still at work, as can be seen when world leaders such as Donald Trump talked about the 'criminality' of migrants trying to enter the southern border of the United States or described sub-Saharan Africa as being made up of 'shithole' countries.[7]

And they can be seen, too, when most European politicians do all they can to turn away and allow desperate refugees and their children from Syria and sub-Saharan Africa to drown within sight of their shores. The plan of a British Home Secretary, Priti Patel, to legislate to allow the Border Force to turn away the rafts of asylum seekers and their children without fear of prosecution beggars belief for its inhumanity, not to say its possible breach of international law. She wasn't the first Home Secretary to act in this negative way toward immigrants. A recently published paper reluctantly revealed by the government due to pressure from journalists shows that UK governments of all complexions have pursued a hostile and discriminatory policy towards non-white immigrants for over thirty years.

Another example of open racism in a modern context comes from Michelle Obama's autobiography *Becoming*. She describes her experiences helping her husband during his electioneering, months before his election as the first US president 'of colour'. The British author and self-styled humanist Christopher Hitchens attacked her in an article for an almost forgotten thesis she had written 20 years previously when she was a Harvard student. She writes:

He tore into me, suggesting that I had been unduly influenced by black radical thinkers and was a crappy writer.

Hitchens had written: *To describe it as hard to read would be a mistake, the thesis cannot be 'read' at all, in the verb's strict sense. This is because it wasn't written in any known language.*

Michelle Obama says: *I was being painted not merely as an outsider but as fully 'other' and so foreign that my language couldn't be recognised.*

For such criticism against this brilliant woman who was to become America's First Lady within months of Hitchens's article speaks volumes about the profound racism that so clearly still exists in the West.

What, it might be asked, have historic 'prejudice, racism and slavery' to do with African children's malnutrition today? The answer is 'everything'. The prejudiced thinking that clearly exists now has come from how people in the past chose to think about people from Africa and their children. They were viewed as different and 'other' to set them apart and inferior to European 'whites' who continued to see themselves as better and more intelligent than 'people of colour'. This view was the justification for Slavery, the cause of the American Civil War and colonialism, and is the basis for much present-day prejudice between nations and the cause of racism present in every aspect of modern life. Despite an overwhelming body of research and evidence that no country or group of people is superior to any other, racism continues to exist. There are countless millions of species of animals and plants on this planet. But there is, to be quite clear, irrespective of place, class, or colour, just one current species of humanity – homo sapiens. Analysis of DNA in different racial groups shows no fundamental difference between them. Every so-called 'difference' between peoples has been brought about by man's propensity to judge and exploit others.

The picture of continuous and worsening harm being 'institutionally' caused by the rich countries did not end with Slavery. It has involved the more recent and determined actions and policies pursued by the West, which have further aggravated children's predicament.

The full extent of family poverty in southern Africa is not well enough appreciated. But to mention that the combined GDPs of over 40 countries in sub-Saharan Africa is less than that of Belgium demonstrates the enormous economic gulf between the affluent West and southern Africa.

The cumulative and destructive effect of events and decisions by the West, like hammer blows, one following another, has caused the adverse social and economic conditions across sub-Saharan Africa that have led to child malnutrition reaching the levels that exist today. Time after time, Africa and Africans have been regarded as counting for nothing – just a valuable source of profit for Western countries who have repeatedly shown no regard or compassion for the well-being of their citizens or, most significantly, its children.

With few exceptions, and despite the often-admirable words of European leaders, little has ever been done to fundamentally tackle the underlying causes of continent-wide poverty and its inevitable consequences – child malnutrition and child deaths. Although worthy of their intentions, campaigns such as 'Red Letter' days, 'Children in Need' and 'Comic Relief' haven't scratched the surface of child poverty and malnutrition. They also risk being pointless exercises to salve the consciences of donors and programme-makers who might think their efforts, however bizarre or outdated, make a meaningful or relevant difference there. One rather extreme such initiative in Uganda is that of an American church-based organisation, 'Watoto Villages', which continues to believe, contrary to all the evidence, that institutional and 'orphanage' care offers any proper response to the problems that African families are undoubtedly facing. Watoto thinks that, due to its work, 'future African leaders' will be produced. They say this justifies their recruitment into orphanages of children who often are not orphans and still have parents. What has caused African parents to be so vulnerable and prey to organisations like Watoto is the predictable consequence of decades of systematic looting and pillage of the continent by the West.

Slavery continued to be highly damaging to African families well into the 19th century and decades beyond its being made illegal in 1833 in Britain and 1865 in the USA, after the defeat of the Confederate States, who had fought the Civil War on the very issue of Slavery. The era of Western colonialism, which was to cause so much harm to the African subcontinent, did not make its entry until the century's last decade, with one significant and nauseating exception – that being in Congo, the region's largest country.

What happened there stemmed accidentally from the worldwide reputation that David Livingstone had earned due to his explorations across the African continent. Livingstone, born in 1813, had been raised in impoverished circumstances in Blantyre in Scotland. After leaving school at age 10, he worked in a cotton mill where working conditions and wages were deplorable. Despite these unlikely circumstances, where he might more obviously have turned his attention to improving the lot of his fellow workers, he became interested in medical missionary work as what he believed was the best means of helping others in the wider world. In doing this, he was inspired by his father and several other religious leaders. After years of medical and evangelical training, he was sent in 1841 to what is now Botswana as a medical missionary with the London Missionary Society. This became the starting point for his lifelong travels across the African continent. In the record of his work and published in 1874 as *The life and African Explorations of David Livingstone*, he is described as:

> *One of a rare breed of men who have modestly imagined they were but instruments in the hands of a Superior Power through whom some of his beneficent designs were to be accomplished.*

While Western explorers and missionaries, such as Livingstone, travelled across Africa in the 18th and 19th centuries, ostensibly to improve the lot of its people, life for most working people in Europe was extremely miserable. This was true of the workers who toiled alongside David Livingstone at Henry Monteith's cotton mill in Scotland, but it was also the case right across Victorian industrial Britain. No better evidence of this comes from the meticulous research carried out in Northern England's towns by Friederich Engels. He was the son of a German manufacturer but wanted to find out about working conditions in Britain. In 1846, during the first of Livingstone's missionary journeys to Africa, Engels published a book in Germany that has had a more substantial impact on the world than all of Livingstone's African travels. It was entitled *The Condition of the Working Class in England*. He had carried out this detailed study in England's industrial centres on his own initiative, not knowing that its shockingly critical findings would have such an impact and be highly influential in the later writings of Karl Marx – the architect of communism. Engels was Hegelian by inclination and thus optimistic about the human condition. Like Dickens before him, he was appalled by what he found about the poverty and privations suffered by working families, especially those employed in the mills and factories of Northern England. He wrote in these harrowing terms:

> *The social order makes family life almost impossible for the worker. In a comfortless, filthy house, hardly good enough for mere nightly shelter, ill-furnished, often neither rain tight nor warm, a foul-smelling atmosphere filling rooms overcrowded with human beings, no domestic comfort is possible.*

Engels concluded his findings with these compelling words:

> *When society places hundreds of proletarians in such a position that they inevitably meet too early a death and an unnatural death, and when*

it deprives thousands of the necessaries of life and places them under conditions in which they cannot live, and knows that these thousands of victims must perish, and yet permits these conditions to remain, its deed is murder, not mere manslaughter, but murder.[8]

'How is it possible,' he continued, 'under such conditions for the lower class to be healthy and long-lived? What else can be expected than excessive mortality, an unbroken series of epidemics, and a progressive deterioration in the physique of the working population?'

He refers, tellingly, to the consequences of malnutrition on children:

Children who are half-starved, just when they most need adequate and nutritious food, must inevitably become weak, scrofulous and rachitic to a high degree. And the neglect to which the great mass of working men's children are condemned leaves ineradicable traces and brings the enfeeblement of the whole race of workers. Add to this the unsuitable clothing of this class, the impossibility of precautions against the cold, and the all too common lack of all medical assistance, and we have a rough idea of the English working class's sanitary condition.

It is hard to imagine a more devastating account of the circumstances of British working-class people than this. It is all the more significant coming from someone who would have known how German workers were treated at the time.

In the face of such evidence of the dreadful privations endured by working people in Britain, including his own family, we might question why Livingstone should think it made any sense *To take civilisation and Christianity to Africa.*

However, he did precisely that. With the reputation that his travels and writing produced, it was no surprise that the story of his being lost should have excited enormous interest and concern. It took another remarkable, if very flawed, man, Henry Morton Stanley, to rise to the challenge of finding Livingstone. His efforts to do this in 1871 became legendary and propelled Stanley into the spotlight of world opinion.

Stanley has been described as 'Africa's Greatest Explorer'. On his return to America and Europe, he was in huge demand as a speaker and authority on all things to do with Africa.

Stanley meeting Livingstone in 1871 at Ujiji in Tanganyika

He wrote, famously but entirely deceitfully, about Africa in the *New York Herald* and to the *Daily Telegraph*, where he stated:

It is not the mere preacher who is wanted here – it is the practical Christian tutor, who can teach people how to become Christians, cure their diseases, construct dwellings, understand agriculture, and can turn his hand to anything – he must be tied to no Church or sect, but be inspired by liberal principles, charity to all men, and devout faith in God.[9]

'Such a man or men,' Stanley said, 'King Mutesa of Uganda invites to come to him. Stanley's statement was based on what he must have known to be flimsy evidence, given that King Mutesa had hundreds of wives and had sold some of his captives to Arab slavers. But even then, it seems that Stanley had started to have ideas about the future possibility of Uganda becoming a British colony. Stanley continued his journeyings in Africa after this momentous meeting with Livingstone. Still, after several years he returned to Europe and gave talks about his travels and experiences in central Africa.

In 1878 a fateful meeting took place between him and representatives of King Leopold II of Belgium, which led to one of the most destructive episodes ever to affect Africa. For several years, Leopold, ruler of one of Europe's smaller and least significant countries, had been intrigued by reports of Congo's mineral and natural riches and wondered whether this might be an opportunity for him and Belgium to play a much larger part on the world's stage. Leopold thought Stanley might help him realise this vision, and after some further overtures, Stanley agreed to visit Belgium to meet the King. Within a year, Stanley decided to work for Leopold, who agreed to finance and arm another expedition by Stanley to Congo. Although it was said to be primarily philanthropic in intent, from the outset, it was evident to be always about money-making, drawing on the wealth Leopold knew would be there for the taking. It included the money to be made from killing elephants for their ivory, then even more prized than now. The enterprise was, from the start, planned to disguise its real purpose. Leopold pretended that he hoped to achieve 'a *confederation of free negro republics*,' mainly to reassure Americans. Written exchanges between Leopold and Stanley made it clear that no delegation of power to local chiefs would ever be allowed.

In the ensuing years, Stanley took responsibility for exploring the Congo River basin and constructing the railway and roads to form the infrastructure for Leopold's commercial exploitation of the 2 million square miles of the hinterland, then called the Congo Free State. Nevertheless, even Stanley, the hardened journalist, was taken in and outwitted by the deceitfulness of his paymaster. The extent of Leopold's ambitions and greed is neither believable nor his duplicity and dishonesty. On one occasion, after being presented by Leopold with the Grand Cross of the Congo, Stanley eulogised King Leopold in a speech to a meeting in Belgium of the Anti-Slavery Conference in these cloying terms:

> *If Royal Greatness consists in the wisdom and goodness of a sovereign leading his people with the solicitude of a shepherd watching over his flock, then the greatest sovereign is your own.*[10]

What Leopold did was mislead the entire world that his business in Congo was a work of humanitarian value to the people of that country designed to bring the benefits of industry and commerce when, in fact, it was about the cruel and revolting exploitation of a kind that was to shock even the worldliest outsiders. He was so glib that he was even appointed as honorary president of the Aborigines Protection Society, a long-established British human rights organisation, while being responsible for the grossest of outrages on the rubber tree plantations' workers at the heart of one of his most profitable enterprises. On these plantations, workers were made to meet unrealistic targets for collecting wild rubber, an essential product for Europe and North America's new motor industries. If they could not produce their quotas, they were liable to have their hands, noses, and ears cut off and exhibited to others as gruesome warnings.

Almost as concerning as this horrific and brutal example of the punishment meted out to African workers was the devastating impact that forced labour practices had on the families of local people who, without their menfolk, were unable to give sufficient attention to growing their food and feeding their children, many of whom died from starvation. This episode was not the only occasion when European businesses, in pursuit of profit in Africa, caused enduring harm to families and children. Leopold never visited Congo, leaving these cruel practices to his officials (Gerhart and Hochschild, 1999).[10]

There can be few worse examples of Colonial exploitation than those under King Leopold's regime. During the period of Belgian rule, the population of Congo collapsed from between 20 and 30 million to less than 9 million in 1911

The punishment meted out to workers by King Leopold's supervisors. This man is looking at his son's foot and ankle, which had been severed to teach him a lesson. Later both his child and wife were killed.

as a result of the starvation, rape, and murders caused by the King Leopold regime's cruel methods and its brutal insistence on workers having to leave their own families and children to cope without them. News of the atrocities was eventually reported to the West, and public disgust of what had been happening in Congo started to mount in Europe and America. Campaigns famously led by E. D. Morel and Roger Casement eventually resulted in the Belgian Government taking over responsibility from Leopold and led to the Belgian Congo replacing the Belgian Free State. Although the most grotesque of the cruelties ended due to this transition to civil administration and accountable Government, it still left a situation that was entirely about Belgium and colonialists' interests rather than being of any benefit whatever to the Congolese.

When what is now the Democratic Republic of Congo became an independent country in 1960, the vast majority of the 200.000 Belgian citizens who had been working in the country until then and who had been filling almost all the posts of public servants shamelessly left within weeks, leaving that country with few qualified citizens to run the new Government and administer services. During the 75 years of the Belgian era, just 16 native Congolese were allowed to attend University, and none had been trained as doctors or engineers. Such was the lack of regard shown, so blatantly and so recently, by these European settlers, used to the benefits of life as privileged Whites towards their African subjects.

Although much international attention and criticism focused on the Belgian Congo, the exploitation of Africans in the region was not confined to that country. Similar and more recent examples of methods of murderously forced labour were reported in French Equatorial Africa, Portuguese-ruled Angola and Mozambique, and German-ruled Cameroon. In Angola, the Portuguese introduced a system called 'contract labour', which was, in reality, 'forced labour' A report on this which the Portuguese government commissioned in1947, estimated that over 40 per cent of the men employed in this compulsory system died as a consequence of its brutality. The author of this report, Captain Galvao, was imprisoned for refusing to cover up the government's duplicity. The Portuguese used forced labour from its colonies as recently as 1959 to feed the mining-based economy of South Africa, financed mainly by holding companies based in Britain and the United States.

The rates of depopulation loss in Angola and Mozambique, through starvation, hostage-taking, the burning of villages, and forced labour, were as severe as in Belgian Congo. The implicit message from all of this was stark: *Making money for Western countries was far more important than Africans and their children's lives.*

It is this period, extending over decades, that the deliberate and callous exploitation by the West of African men, women, and children right across West Africa – amounted to crimes against humanity – and make the case that it was this same era that reinforced the crucial foundations of racism and prejudices first built by slavery and directed at Africa and Africans that has continued to the present time.

A British but much less well-known example of this total lack of concern for African lives can be seen in the era of Lord Leverhulme's palm oil plantations in Congo. Leverhulme, a Lancashire entrepreneur, is still described by some present-day British businessmen as 'an enlightened businessman and philanthropist.' However, his overtly racist and patronising views about Africans hardly differed from those of Burton or Leopold. He believed that Africans were primitive, barbaric, and ignorant and that it was a blessing for them to have been colonised by the leading nations of the North. He says:

The African native will be happier, produce the best, and live under the larger conditions of prosperity when his labour is directed and organised by his white brother, who has all these millions of years start ahead of him.

This lack of technologies in Africa and Asia had permitted many colonisers to judge them as backwards and needing Western interference, even though technology can hardly be a complete or adequate measure of civilised society.

William Hesketh Lever's soap manufacturing company, Lever Brothers, became interested in palm oil's potential as a profitable soap ingredient and bought massive estates in Congo. Although Lever's company did not employ the worst callous practices Leopold used, it is clear that it used the Belgian system of forced labour – known as *'travail force'*, which also did great harm to the well-being of families and children. The company was later accused by Jules Marchal, an ex-Belgian diplomat, of *'Causing more deaths than the Nazi Holocaust.'* He puts the number of Congolese, mainly children, who lost their lives because of famine during the Lever era at more than 10 million.[11]

The harsh methods used by Lever Brothers and Unilever continued in Congolese prisons right until 1959, in contrast to the much fairer practices for producing the palm oil used in Nigeria, where people's rights to land were more adequately respected. Unlike the Congo, they were allowed to benefit from their hard work, whereas right until the end of WW2, children as young as ten were still working in the Lever Brothers palm oil estates.

Lever felt, bizarrely, that he had a duty to impose his methods on the native population in Congo because Africans themselves weren't taking the opportunity to make profits. He believed it was his responsibility to do so. When there were insurrections about his methods and the impact they were having on families and children and the patterns and structures of traditional society, his company, in one instance, locked up all the women in retaliation. In another case, a revolt was brought under control, but with such brutality, over a thousand deaths resulted.

Lord Lever's reputation has escaped lightly from the vicious regimes he and his company inflicted on African workers. Even recently, there have been attempts to sanitise his work – most egregiously by British academic Brian Lewis – who seems to believe that he was just a remarkable businessman, not untypical of his kind in Victorian England.[12] But it is impossible not to see Lever as an out-and-out racist and white supremacist. Like many other businessmen and colonialists bent on their mission to make as much money as possible, he seemed unaware that the origin of the species 'homo sapiens' was found thousands of years earlier in Africa. and that all so-called 'white brothers' have African genes in their DNA. He was also ignorant or suspicious of the tangible evidence of earlier African history and the achievements of previous generations of Africans, which had long preceded and frequently surpassed those of Europeans.

Jules Marchal, who had been very critical of King Leopold's tyrannical methods in Congo, knew Lever, and in correspondence with him, Lever wrote:

> *It would serve no useful purpose for the white man to go and try to reverse the Divine order under which intellect and mental power rules and develops, protects and benefits inferior nations'*[13]

In contrast even with the British Colonial Office's views, Lever's extraordinary beliefs were that entrepreneurs like him had a right to take land from their African owners simply because he had: The *ability and willingness to profit from God's earth and that the world's land ought to be in possession of those who can develop it and its resources.*

That kind of certainty disqualifies him from ever being described as a philanthropist.

His lack of insight into what his work had achieved can be seen in this extraordinary extract from his company magazine 'Bubbles' which he wrote in 1919 after the end of WW1

> *We face the future with eyes that gleam with triumph tasted and throb with the ambition to make Great Britain and the Empire not only the greatest Empire the world has seen but also the Empire that contains the greatest number of happy men and women in which each citizen has the fullest opportunity for the attainment of happiness, comfort and prosperity.*

Far from being benevolent, as still often portrayed, William Lever must rank as one of the worst examples of Victorian greed and ambition, fired by an arrogant belief in his enterprise's moral and 'Divine' purpose.

Modern-day Africans writing subsequently about Lever's work in Congo make no secret of their abomination of his condescending and racist attitudes, portraying them as lesser humans, unworthy of respect.

Lever's company, Lever Brothers, became Unilever in 1929 and one of the largest companies in Europe. As Lord Leverhulme, his name is marked by the prestigious Lady Lever Museum and Art Gallery, which he endowed at Port Sunlight, coincidentally, just a few miles from Liverpool, the city where many of its business leaders had been actively complicit in the British slave trade several decades earlier. There was no mention, until recently, at the Art Gallery at Port Sunlight of the wholly exploitative basis of Lever's fortune. This may, it seems, be changing, and the gallery's website now does at least begin to acknowledge that his plantations did rely on the appalling cruelties of forced labour.

Those who profited most from slavery and aggressive colonialism, such as the Lascelles family and Lever Brothers, have gone to great lengths to distance themselves from their predecessors' cruel and self-serving activities. Their websites gloss over the scale of involvement their predecessors had in slavery and exploitation instead of openly acknowledging the suffering they caused to millions of Africans, let alone offering anything like the level of reparation that might be appropriate, especially as in these examples, in Leeds and Liverpool respectively, there are large numbers of poor people of African origin living close to their extravagant properties,

Perhaps conscious of its own very chequered history, Unilever has tried to affirm its current humane ethos and values.

Advertisement for Lever Brothers Sunlight Soap

However, even that company has not been free from legitimate accusations of racism in their inept advertising of Dove soap within the last decade. In its ill-considered 'Campaign for Real Beauty', it unwittingly suggested in an advertisement on Facebook in 2017 that 'dirty' people of colour could be purified to white with soap. As a consequence, Unilever had to issue a public apology. Nor can the company's current profits and lavish offices be squared with the fact that the raw materials for many of its sophisticated products are still grown in countries in Africa by farmers and workers on low incomes and where child malnutrition and death rates are sky-high. When Independence did take place in Congo in 1960, as mentioned earlier, most of the Belgians, holding nearly all the jobs in public services there, couldn't get away fast enough. This behaviour speaks volumes about how this one insignificant and tiny Western country felt about the citizens of its immensely profitable

African province, more than 77 times larger. They, self-evidently, couldn't care less about what the future might hold for their former servants and employees, let alone their children.

During the later decades of the nineteenth century, and possibly inspired by King Leopold's example, other European nations became interested in exploiting the commercial benefits that could be wrested from West Africa and the Congo Basin. This was demonstrated by this extraordinary extract from a leader in the *Daily Telegraph* in October 1884:

> *Leopold 11 has knit adventurers, traders and missionaries of many races into one band of men, under the most illustrious of travellers (H.M.Stanley) to carry new ideas into the interior of Africa of law, order, humanity, and protection of the natives.*

France, Germany, Portugal, and Britain sent missions and gunboats to claim parts of this region, including Togo, Namibia, Cameroon, Angola, DRC, and Congo. These initial forays would become a continent-wide competition between the more prominent nations – France, Germany, Spain, Portugal and Britain, all entertaining ambitious plans to exercise power over parts of the continent, especially France in North and West Africa, Germany in East and South-West Africa, and Britain across the entirety of eastern Africa right from the Mediterranean to the tip of Southern Africa.

During this era, it became clear that the developing race between European countries was in danger of getting out of control, even to the point of excluding Germany, whose own territorial ambitions were at risk. There is no need to detail the crisscrossing claims for land other than to make the point that Africans themselves were never invited to play any part at all in the discussions or the decision-making that followed. All Western nations' stance seemed to be that Africans should not have any say in these matters and that it was the West's right to make whatever decisions best suited their commercial and strategic interests. The term 'The Scramble for Africa' described the entire process. It is worth emphasising that this was debated and decided in Berlin as recently as 1884/5, not in some long distant past.

After months of debate and argument, Africa's map was crudely redrawn to show how Britain, France, Germany, Belgium (as Leopold 11), Portugal, Turkey and Spain would arbitrarily divide most of the continent. Yet to come to Africa and as particularly violent aggressors were Italy and the Boers. Such

Dividing up Africa – Berlin Conference 1885

behaviour on the part of the so-called civilised Europeans did not augur at all well for Africa's peoples, as will be clear from these examples.

In crudely dividing the subcontinent by sitting around tables in Germany, the Europeans had little or no information about the geographical or climactic characters of the countries they were about to create, let alone about the ethnicities and beliefs of the peoples who already lived there or about the soils and potential for growing crops. The Europeans were ignorant about the rich cultures and complex forms of public administration, such as those in Ethiopia, Ghana and Nigeria, which had existed for centuries before their arrival. Lord Salisbury admitted that the British negotiators at Berlin had no idea where it made sense to create new national boundaries. These artificial boundaries took no note, for example, of ethnic groups but became consolidated after these newly formed countries became independent nations sixty years later.

It is not surprising that such an uninformed approach led to frequent economic and political problems and severe social and ethnic tensions, such as those that erupted so murderously in Rwanda many decades later due to Belgian incompetence.

Kenya

The methods used by Britain in settling or 'pacifying' Kenya were notoriously vicious. Kenya has a more equable climate than many other parts of Africa, making it particularly attractive to settlers who came in increasing numbers in the first decades of the twentieth century, encouraged by fertile farming land promises. By 1915 more than a million acres had been taken over by just a thousand colonialists, keen to purchase prime agricultural land at giveaway prices. Lord Delamere, who became one of the leading landholders in Kenya, reputedly bought 100,000 acres of lush farmland near Mount Kenya for a penny an acre. Kenya's manifestation as some kind of Nirvana for settlers was later shown to the world in romantic terms in films such as 'Out of Africa' or in sentimental and Anglo-centric books such as Elspeth Huxley's 'Flame Trees of Thika'. This process was naturally opposed by the native African peoples who had traditionally farmed these lands. British forces violently countered their objections and killed many thousands of them using machine guns where they considered it necessary.

One young officer recorded in his diary the day after his unit had killed over 1000 Africans that still more violence – or as he wrote: *'Hammering'* – *might be needed to teach others a lesson*. When news of these killings returned to London, a young civil servant – Winston Churchill – questioned whether such murderous methods could be justified. But even his comments were ignored.

One of the methods in Kenya to deal with local opposition protesting at the takeover of their lands was the introduction of taxes, requiring Africans to pay a house tax to the colonial power. This policy led to many families becoming impoverished and starved. Some tribal groups were particularly challenging to subdue, one being the Masai. In that instance, the colonial Government introduced a scheme that forcibly removed young Masai from their homes and trained them as tax collectors of their peoples. This inglorious British rule laid the foundations for further Kenyan insurrection in the run-up five decades later to Kenyan Independence. During that period, the British Government once again used brutal force to kill, torture and maim thousands of Kenyans who protested their right to self-government. Spurious statistics and stories were used in the British press to represent the Mau-Mau as murderous killers of innocent white settlers. However, the facts, as meticulously researched by Caroline Elkins, an American Pulitzer Prize-winning academic and journalist, paint a very different picture. She reports how just 63 police and soldiers were killed in the conflict, compared to more than 11,000 Kenyans, some of whom were stripped naked before being murdered. Others were tortured, and many women were raped.[13]

The UK Government opposed class actions brought in the courts more recently by survivors of these violent events. But when secret files which revealed the brutality which had been officially sanctioned during the British occupation of Kenya were discovered at the Foreign and Commonwealth Office's record store at Hanslope Park in Buckinghamshire, it became impossible for Britain to maintain its lack of frankness about how it had cruelly treated so many Kenyan citizens, or to disguise the lengths they had gone to cover up the conduct of its colonial administrators.

In her book, *One Long Night*,[14] about the history of concentration camps, another American journalist, Andrea Pitzer, describes the treatment of Kenyan citizens who were suspected of supporting the Mau Mau, as being reminiscent in its callous brutality of the methods used by Germany in the concentration camps of WW2 with guards allowed to torture, gang rape and even murder without sanction. She adds that the colonial administration's Attorney General wrote to the Governor in 1957 instructing that prisoners should not be struck on the kidneys, spleen or liver. He wrote disgracefully: *If we are to sin, we must sin quietly*. One 82-year-old Kenyan, Wambugu Wa Nyingi, who appeared as a plaintiff in the eventual court proceedings in London in 2009, has added to his testimony this moving and remarkably restrained address to the Queen:

> *I want the world to know about the years I have lost and what was taken away from a generation of Kenyans. If I could speak to the Queen, I would say that Britain did many good things in Kenya, but they also did many bad things. The settlers took our land, killed our people, and burned our houses. In the years before Independence, people were beaten, their land was stolen, women were raped, men were castrated, and their children were killed. I do not hold her responsible, but I would like the wrongs done to other Kenyans and me to be recognised by the British Government so I can die in peace.*

Aside from an apology to the victims of torture and the announcement of a modest compensation fund for them made in 2013 by William Hague, the then Foreign Secretary, about the behaviour of British Imperial Officers during the Mau Mau emergency, no broader apology or compensation has ever been offered by the UK anywhere else. To emphasize the thinking of the UK government, it was stated that the response wasn't to be seen as precedence for any other colonial administration.

Other secret records, recently discovered in Kenya and not yet published, have revealed the extent of the collaboration of several highly respected NGOs. They willingly worked with the colonial government to paint African protesters as terrorists rather than legitimate advocates for Kenyan Independence. What these organisations did was to assist the colonial authorities in attempting to change how local communities saw Mau Mau freedom fighters who had been arrested and imprisoned. They did this by working with the Kenyan Women's Association, Maendeleo Ya Wanawake (MYMO) and the Christian Council of Kenya (CCK) to attempt to subvert black resistance in concentration camps as well as in slums and shantytowns by offering 'pastoral care' which had far more to do with the agenda of the Government than with the legitimate aspiration of Kenyan citizens for autonomy. These records reveal the full extent of the colonial Government's readiness to try to change Kenyan citizens' hearts and minds about the movement for Independence. They also demonstrate the surprising and previously unknown willingness of these globally respected NGOs to offer their active assistance in this disreputable process, in stark contrast to their reputations as organisations set up to save lives and support parents and children in crises.

Caroline Elkins describes how her study revealed: ' *How a society warped by racism can descend into casual inhumanity.*' That judgement could still stand as a fair comment on how Britain, over long periods, acted in its colonies.

Kenya is now a popular destination for millions of Western tourists. They can enjoy its fabulous Indian Ocean beaches or visit its many beautiful game parks, such as Masai Mara. Here is the spectacular annual migration of thousands of wildebeests to find better grazing land after the hot season's lack of rain. Despite the income this industry generates, the proportion of children under five who are stunted remains at well over 30 per cent and increases yearly. A crucial review of progress towards ending child stunting by a research group led by Zulfiqar Bhutta[21] showed that sub-Saharan African countries, including Kenya, lag behind other comparable regions where more significant achievements have been made over the last 30 years. This is partly because of inadequate investment in the 'drivers' that make a difference, including primary education for girls, tackling poverty, and better health services in more rural areas. (More recently, Kenya has been working to improve the well-being of its children through its involvement with the UN. The results of these efforts are encouraging, as described later.)

Ghana

Records confirm that the area of West Africa, now known as Ghana (previously the Gold Coast), had a long-standing history of trading with nations as far as China. It was at the heart of gold production and gold working for centuries. For a time around the Middle Ages, Ghana and surrounding countries such as today's Mali were the sources of two-thirds of the world's gold. The wealth generated from gold mining led to some of the region's leaders becoming fabulously wealthy, a history reflected even today in ceremonies and celebrations where gold dominates participants' dress and their cavalcades. These can still be seen in the rituals of the Ashanti Kingdom of Ghana. In 1995 the gold-based wealth of these leaders was famously displayed at the Silver Jubilee celebrations of King Otumfuo Ware 11 in Kumasi in the presence of some 75,000 of his loyal subjects in the most extravagant display of royal regalia to be seen anywhere. Among the most precious of these gold artefacts was the Royal Stool, a sacred object that could only by tradition be seen in public four times a century.

Whilst in the Gold Coast in 1900, Britain had been using less aggressive methods of control than in East Africa, the Governor, Frederick Hodgson, demanded that the stool be brought to him as the representative of The Queen to demonstrate his importance and superiority over the Ashanti peoples and their rulers. This was a conspicuous error of judgment and led to two decades of unrest and hostility, which caused hundreds of deaths and the forced exile of Nana Prempeh, the King of Ghana.

This episode was less dreadful than the years of murderously oppressive colonial rule in Kenya. Nonetheless, it demonstrates how much colonialists were ignorant and disrespectful of the tradition and beliefs that mattered in Africa. The affair even caused David Lloyd George to censure the Colonial Office for its inhumane attitude towards the Asante people. However, there were no significant improvements in how Britain treated Ghanaians in the decades before independence in 1957. Health service provision for citizens was far worse than for expatriates.

Before then, seven hospitals catered for 3000 expatriates in the Gold Coast region compared to thirty-six hospitals for 4 million Africans. Significantly few young people were able to enter secondary education due to lack of provision, let alone not being encouraged to go to Universities by the British government. Education was similarly neglected in terms of school places and how the schools for African students were forced to use English textbooks about English history, geography, and even English weather and ways of life.

South Africa

The story of Western colonisation in South Africa is more complicated than in most of Africa, made particularly so by the battles for power between the British and the Boer communities, leading to South Africa's partition. The Griquas were caught up in this, a group of mixed-race, semi-nomadic and Dutch-speaking people who had chosen to live on land with indeterminate boundaries near the Orange River.

One of the events that shaped South Africa and transformed its economy was discovering gold and diamonds in what was termed 'The Reef', a geological formation in an area around Kimberly where various native groups, including the Griquas, had traditionally lived. Realising that these deposits were of potentially high value caused an enormous inrush of entrepreneurs and miners determined to make their fortunes. The cruel way the Griqua peoples and their families were treated after these discoveries is further testimony to how Europeans were ready to disregard local populations' views and interests when making choices regarding their opinions. Decades of arguments and conflict regarding the Griqua peoples' rights made life extraordinarily difficult for them, made worse by the racist and threatening policies of the apartheid era.

South West Africa (now Namibia)

Around the turn of the nineteenth century, German settlers, encouraged by their Government, moved into SW Africa and started to farm, even though these lands were already used by two indigenous groups of pastoralists – the Nama and the Herero. Between 1896 and 1903, the number of colonial settlers increased from 2,000 to 4,700, taking rights, land and animals from the pastoralists. This invasion had followed one of the worst outbreaks of rinderpest which had reduced the indigenous groups to abject subjugation, and they were forced to accept employment as labourers. Although the then German Governor, Theodore von Leutwein, reported this to Berlin as evidence of the 'good sense' of the pastoralists and is said to have treated them with politeness. The same was not true of the settlers, who commonly resorted to brutal floggings and rape without judicial retribution. Even murders went unpunished.

In 1904 the Herero responded violently to the treatments and humiliations that had been meted out to them and attacked several isolated farms killing more than 100 German farmers, many of whom were mutilated and tortured. No women or children were harmed. However, in reprisal for this, a German army group led by General von Trotha moved into the area. He gave the Herero people an ultimatum – 'expulsion or extermination.' After fencing off the uninhabitable Namib desert from the farmed area, 8000 men and 16000 women and children were left between the wire and the German guns. Just 5000 managed to escape, but most died of starvation in the desert or camps or were killed. This reprisal campaign continued for years until, in 1911, it was reported that less than a quarter of the entire Herero and Nama population had survived. South West Africa was a defeated country and wide open to settlement by Germans – as illustrated today by most of its towns' German names – until and since the country became independent Namibia in 1990.

General von Trotha left for Germany in 1905 and was rewarded with the Order of Merit for his 'Services to the Fatherland.' After this episode, awful as it was, the remaining Africans were compelled to work for meagre wages or none on cotton plantations until they rebelled against this. This led to further uprisings from local people in what became known as the Maji-Maji rebellion, in which they believed they would be untouched by German bullets. Not surprisingly, this was not the case. The military response by armed troops led to the near extermination of all indigenous people across a large swathe of Namibia and parts of the present day and largely unpopulated Selous game reserve of southern Tanzania. It has been recently estimated that more than 150,000 indigenous people died either from starvation or killing. It has been described as 'The first genocide of the twentieth century.'

Even this dreadful saga at the hands of Germany did not end the persecution of Namibian citizens. During the apartheid era, the South African Government, which had territorial ambitions for South West Africa, ruthlessly tried to impose its policies. It was not until 1990 that Namibia emerged as a wholly independent country free from the turmoil of almost a century of foreign dominance and ruthless exploitation. The country is one of the world's most sparsely populated, second only in that respect to Mongolia. Although by no means as poor as some of its neighbours, as a result of the discovery of rich mineral deposits, including uranium, it still has significant social and economic problems arising from an inadequate supply of clean water and sewerage, which caused high levels of infant deaths, especially in poorer families as a result of diarrhoea arising from these poor standards of hygiene and sanitation.

In Namibia, the prevalence of stunting amongst children under five years of age stands currently at 23.1 per cent. Although lower than for some comparable countries in the region, it is still extraordinarily high for a country enjoying such high levels of wealth and resources. This is just one example of the continued racism and exploitation in former colonies even after their independence, especially when there were scarce mineral resources.

The Herero and Name genocides story is not just of consequence as an unheeded precursor to the calamities that would befall Europe in the twentieth century. David Olusoga describes it as:

> *Neither a historical cudgel to beat Germany and the German inhabitants of Namibia nor force them to accept guilt for their forebears' crimes. On the contrary, it is of consequence in and for itself. To the descendants of its victims, the genocides are not a distant memory but have been described as 'an open wound that shapes their day to day existence. (Olusoga & Erichsen, 2010).*[15]

These brief accounts of Western involvements in countries across a cross-section of sub-Saharan Africa speak for themselves. Whether in Congo, South Africa, Ghana, South West Africa or Kenya, the examples illustrate the grotesque one-sidedness of the relationship. The colonisers' interests were always about the profits to be obtained from their colonies and never about how they might contribute to their development. I can find no evidence that children in any of the countries in sub-Saharan Africa have ever significantly benefitted from colonialism – however measured. Conversely, millions of children in every country continue to suffer from decades of European exploitation. They remain poor and suffer from malnutrition and poor health precisely because Europeans treated their forebears unfairly and cruelly. Leander Heldring and James Robinson examined the evidence of colonialism's overall impact in several published papers. They concluded that, despite many claims to the contrary, Africa's development was retarded by the effect of over two decades of colonialism (Heldring & Robinson, 2012).[16]

The destructive long-term impact on children needs little further emphasis or detailing. It reveals the colonisers' callous indifference right into the twentieth century towards African communities – women and children included.

As a final comment about Western colonialism, it is worth quoting Albert Schweitzer, the 1952 Nobel peace prize laureate. He had spent the latter half of his remarkable life as a missionary doctor in Gabon, formerly in French Equatorial Africa. Although he cannot be called a progressive, he wrote:

Who can describe the injustices and cruelties that they (Africans)have suffered at the hands of Europeans in the course of a lifetime? …If a record could be compiled of all that has happened between the white and coloured races, it would make a book containing numbers of pages that the reader would have to turn over unread because their contents would be too horrible.

In a powerful and visionary sermon he delivered in 1905 before going as a doctor to Africa, he said:

Our culture divides people into two classes; civilised men, a title bestowed on the persons who do the classifying, and others who have only the human form and who may perish or go to the dogs for all the 'civilised' men care. Oh, this noble culture of ours! It speaks so piously of human dignity and human rights and then disregards this dignity and these human rights and treads them underfoot, only because they live overseas, or because their skins are of a different colour or because they cannot help themselves. This culture does not know how hollow and miserable and full of glib talk it is. This culture has no right to speak of personal dignity and human rights. Think of the atrocities that were perpetrated upon people made subservient to us, how systematically we have ruined them with our alcoholic gifts and everything else we have done …We decimate them and then, by the stroke of a pen, we take their land so that they have nothing left at all.

So when you speak about our missions, let this be your message: We must make atonement for all the crimes we read about in the newspapers. We must also make atonement for the worse ones that we do not read about in the newspapers, 'the terrible crimes that are shrouded in the jungle night'.[17]

Each of these separate country accounts demonstrates so graphically just how the Western powers continued to take advantage of the vulnerability of African nations and their peoples not long after the end of slavery. The colonial period extended for more than fifty years, right up to the independence movements of the twentieth century when Africans started to assert their rights to self-government. Instead of selling their peoples into slavery, the West then made money by robbing them of their natural resources and lands without troubling to make any treaties or even questioning their actions' morality. By using this time primarily to plunder the resources of sub-Saharan Africa and enrich themselves, European nations caused immense damage to African families, especially to their children's health and well-being. The combination of the Atlantic slave trade, followed by the decades of colonisation, was a lethal mix for African children. Their welfare, health and nutrition counted for nothing in the eyes of the Europeans.

Although the League of Nations had adopted a Declaration about the Rights of the Child as early as 1924 to emphasise that all children had an inalienable right to certain rights and liberties, no Western nation or company took any action to make a reality of this in Africa during the colonial era Significantly it was Ghana. which became the first African country to adopt and put into practice the UN Convention on Children's Rights, and, probably no coincidence that it was one of the first African countries to gain its independence (in 1957)

Notes and Further Reading

Although a few historians claim that the Empire's building process was a positive and necessary experience for the Southern hemisphere's colonised countries, they are the exception.

Most modern writers about Africa tell very different stories, with outstanding accounts of how Europeans, including Britain, looted sub-Saharan African counties in the nineteenth and twentieth centuries.

Fanon's *The Wretched of the Earth*[18] written about Algeria is an extraordinarily moving and insightful picture of how colonialism differed from the civilised reality of most Western countries, where it could be taken for granted that citizens had rights and where 'decent' behaviour is the norm. In colonial countries, such as Algeria, rules were enforced by the policeman and the soldier using their rifle butts and napalm to uphold the peace. This is not to say that countries that have become independent after being colonised are models of freedom, but Fanon, who recognised this, provided the most explicit description of what colonisation meant for oppressed peoples. This is one of the most influential books ever written about the full meaning of colonialism and the economic and psychological degradation that Western imperialism inflicted across the Third World a century ago.

Also essential is *King Leopold's Ghost* by Adam Hochschild (1998), described as *The story of King Leopold's ruin of the Congo*. He gives a graphic account of this episode which leaves little room for debate about the brutality of Leopold's rule and the prodigious and unforgivable harm it caused to millions of families and children. Also worth reading and written by a Belgian diplomat, Jules Marchal, is *'Lord Leverhulme's Ghost; Colonial Exploitation in the Congo* (2008). No other scholar has studied colonial forced labour as thoroughly as Marchal has in the Congo or is so well placed to comment about it.

One book that tries, unpersuasively, to give a somewhat more positive account of Lord Leverhulme's work is; *'So Clean; Lord Leverhulme, Soap and Civilisation'* Brian Lewis, 2008. Even this volume clarifies that Lever's methods, not just in Africa but also in Scotland, later in his life when he turned his attention to the fishing industry, were nowhere near 'as clean' as is sometimes represented.

Of great interest are books by Africans about Congo, and especially worthwhile is the highly critical set of essays in *'The Congo from Leopold to Kabila; a People's History'* by Georges Nzongola – Ntalaja, 2002.[19]

This concludes that the only way ahead for Congo, as well as Rwanda, Burundi, and Uganda is to put an end to governments established by force of arms and embark on a path of genuine reconciliation, justice and inclusiveness.

The appalling record of Germany's brutal involvement in South West Africa, today's Namibia, largely overlooked, is documented brilliantly in *The Kaiser's Holocaust; Germany's forgotten Genocide* by David Olusoga and Casper Erichsen (2010.) The Germans tried exterminating two groups of indigenous citizens, a foretaste of what was to come in the subsequent rise of Nazism and the genocide of the Second World War.

It is interesting to see how well-intentioned accounts can become embarrassingly dated. In the then best-selling *'The Scramble for Africa'*[20,] the liberally minded author Thomas Packenham says:

> *In 1880 most of the continent was still ruled by Africans and barely explored. By 1902, five European Powers had grabbed almost the whole*

continent, given themselves 30 new colonies and protectorates, 10 million square miles of new territory, and 110 million bewildered new subjects.'

Packenham points out that Livingstone's famous 3 C's (Commerce, Christianity and Civilisation) soon became 4 in number, with 'Conquest' being added and dominant, mainly by using the Gatling gun. Packenham's approach is surprisingly jingoistic and sometimes reads as a 'Boy's Own' version of colonialism – bizarrely described by one reviewer as a ' delightful account 'and by another as a 'magnificent swashbuckling, blood bolstered epic'.

Chapter 5

Neo-colonialism in sub-Saharan Africa – The last stage of Imperialism

Many formerly colonised African countries achieved their complete independence in the last half of the twentieth century, very often after their determined and persistent efforts. In the case of British colonies, the dates ranged from 1957, when Ghana became independent under its first president Dr Kwame Nkrumah, through to 1990, when, after a prolonged struggle with white Rhodesian separatists, Zimbabwe, at last, became an independent nation, led by Canaan Banana. During the '60s alone, some 13 countries, including Zambia, Tanzania, Nigeria and Kenya, ended their constitutional links with Britain. Although all had made a supposedly complete break with their former colonisers, their independence was quickly compromised by what became known as Neo-Colonialism. Although they were legally separated, their economies were dominated as before from outside, either by their former colonisers or by international companies who negotiated one-sided trading arrangements that constrained their rights as new nations to make their own decisions about policy and strategies. In practice, this meant that they were still subservient to external bodies whose priorities were, as ever, to profit from the resources that had, in theory, transferred back into the ownership and control of the new nations.

It could have been a constructive process for the new countries, given a chance to fully manage their own destinies and make the best use of their natural resources, which were, in many cases, very considerable. According to Dr Nkrumah, Africa had more than 40 per cent of the world's water power, iron reserves twice the size of America's, and 53 of the world's most important industrial metals and minerals. More recent estimates show Africa has more uranium, zirconium, gold, cobalt, copper and industrial diamonds than any other continent. It also has far more potential for solar power than anywhere in the northern hemisphere. However, after independence, Africa was exploited as never before, with the bulk of its natural and mineral resources exported to the West in unfair deals. This process was of little benefit to most African people, especially their families and children.

Much of this profiteering was the responsibility of large institutions such as international tea, sugar and coffee companies, along with Firestone, Nestle, British American Tobacco, BP, Coca-Cola, Unilever and Glencore or by powerful conglomerates of Western companies such as the AngloAmerican Corporation, De Beers, Reynolds Mining, all backed by international bankers based in London, New York, or Frankfurt.

In 1965 Nkrumah published findings such as these in his remarkable and prescient book *Neo-Colonialism The last stage of Imperialism*[1], which caused such consternation in the USA State Department that $25million of US Aid to Ghana was immediately cancelled. He left office in 1968 after a coup that he claimed had been organised by the CIA. Whether this was so is unclear, but if true, he wouldn't have been the first African President to have been forced out of office by American interests. This episode is a graphic example of Western governments' readiness to take whatever steps they chose to maintain their economic stranglehold on African countries. Their involvement in African national politics became much more aggressive during the Cold War. Their overarching concerns were that Russia's influence in Africa threatened their own commercial links, especially with countries with valuable mineral resources. One of the most egregious examples of the involvement of the United States in African affairs around the time of independence was in the Democratic Republic of Congo (DRC). DRC was found to have rich uranium deposits at Shinkolobwe, a heavily guarded mine. Even during WW2, these heavily guarded deposits were mined by European companies. Many Congolese men were forced to work there in hazardous conditions due to the lethally high percentage of active Uranium in the ore. After the end of the world war, when nuclear weapons were being developed, the Americans decided that this mine was of supreme strategic importance to them in their race for weapons supremacy against the Soviet Union. Issues about African sovereignty were not allowed to play any part in their calculations. The CIA played a significant role in how the emergent nations and their elected leaders struggled to plan their futures.

British historian Susan Williams has recently documented this in great detail and persuasively in her book White Malice (Williams, 2021)[2]. She reveals that, whatever America's posturing as a beacon for African nations emerging from the yoke of European colonialism, its own interests always came first, regardless of the price Africans paid. She states that the evidence is clear that President Eisenhower personally authorised the assassination of Patrice Lumumba, the elected President of DRC, whose radical ideas were seen as being at odds with American interests. The USA and, in particular, the CIA played a vital role in replacing him with the corrupt and murderous dictator Joseph-Desire Mobutu, who was to terrorise and impoverish his country for over thirty years.

She provides new evidence and insights into how the CIA went about its mission of clandestinely intervening in African affairs whenever it considered that these might conflict in any way with America's economic, commercial and military strategies. In particular, she describes how the USA took over the mining of high-grade Uranium ore from mines in Congo. This material was crucial to America in developing the first atomic bomb and winning the battle with the USSR about nuclear supremacy.

She also touches on the possible involvement of the CIA in the deaths, in similar circumstances, of Franz Fanon and Paul Robeson, both close friends of President Nkrumah and outspoken advocates of civil and human rights in America and Africa.

Williams's authoritative study of this period presages the different ways in which the USA was later to ignore the interests of African citizens and families, just as cynically as the European powers had done for decades before. (see chapters 3 and 4 for details)

The impoverishment of Africa that had occurred during colonialism did not end with the independence movement of the late twentieth century. The European powers and the United States did not cede economic independence to African leaders as hoped. Instead, they found other ways of controlling their former colonies, mainly by maintaining their financial and security domination of these newly formed and primarily small countries, regardless of the impact on the well-being of African families and children.

Notes and further reading
Neo-Colonialism The last stage of Imperialism Kwame Nkrumah (1965)[1]
Dr Nkrumah was a remarkable President of one of the first African countries to become independent. He was also an impressive writer and intellectual. He foresaw many of the challenges that were to come from Western nations in the wake of their conceding independence to their former colonies.

This landmark study is a powerful and well-researched attack on what he called International Monopoly Capitalism. It describes how companies such as ICI, Anglo-American, Oppenheimer and Rockefeller controlled the extraction of scarce resources from across the sub-continent whilst protecting and enhancing their profits. It is a critical evaluation of how the Western powers and multinational companies dominated Africa's newly independent nations without regard or respect for their new status. In doing this, he incurred much hostility from the West, particularly the USA. They were not prepared or willing to find themselves on the receiving end of criticism, however well-argued and accurate. Nkrumah's comments remain today as a warning about the malignant impact of neo-colonialism across Africa – arguably worse than colonialism itself had been. He was joined in his concerns about neo-colonialism by other leaders, academics and writers. These included Julius Nyerere in Tanzania, Leopold Senghor in Senegal, Sekou Toure in Guinea, and Nnamdi Azikiwe in Nigeria, whose hopes were that Africa should try to overcome the limitations colonialists had imposed on them and work more closely together on Pan African initiatives.

Although there were several promising initiatives, including the setting up of East African Airways and an East African common trading market, these have not stood the test of time. Consequently, Individual African governments have been more exposed and vulnerable to external pressures, mainly, as will be seen, from the World Bank and multinational trading companies.

Neo-Colonialism and the Poverty of 'Development in Africa'. Mark Langan, 2018[2]
In this recent and sophisticated review of Nkrumah's analysis, more than 60 years after it was written. This book is a thorough and gripping account of the foreign policies of the American government and its covert actions through the Central Intelligence Agency (CIA) in Africa during the Cold War period after WW2 and up to the end of colonialism. Langan argues that it has stood the test of time and concludes that it remains a valuable and critical expose of how the West failed to respect African sovereignty to the detriment of their economies and citizens' well-being.

Morris, James(2015) *Oxfam in Kenya, 1963-2002.* PhD thesis,
University of York (Morris, 2015)
Here, the author describes the ambiguous position in which Oxfam was placed before and after Kenyan independence. Whilst not specifying exactly

how Oxfam acted in concert with the Colonial government in dealing with Mau Mau supporters, he outlines how NGOs can and did find themselves conflicted about their roles in the developing world. The broader lesson is that it cannot be taken for granted that the objectives of foreign NGOs are necessarily the same as those of the governments in whose countries they operate.

Chapter 6
The failure of Tropical Medicine to reach out to and benefit developmentally vulnerable African children

Western and especially 'Tropical' medicine was markedly unfit for purpose both in colonial Africa and India during the late nineteenth and much of the twentieth centuries. Its continued failure in the first part of that era contributed directly and indirectly to increased numbers of malnourished children and their deaths. This book could be devoted to the failure of colonial governments and doctors to recognise or admit that the problems of ill health and malnutrition experienced by children in Sub-Saharan Africa and South Asia were more the result of their ill-considered economic and agricultural policies than of endemic disease or any ignorance on the part of the citizens themselves. On occasions, it is clear that, even when the evidence demonstrated this to be the case, efforts were made to suppress the inconvenient facts, such was the defensiveness of the colonial powers.

Several historians and ecologists, including John Ford, Helge Kjekhus, and Pratik Chakrabarti, have documented this picture of colonial and medical arrogance and incompetence.

In writing about the pre-colonial era, John Ford[1] has pointed out that the deadly disease of Trypanosomiasis or sleeping sickness had been effectively contained within prescribed areas when local peoples had created no-mans lands to prevent the disease from spreading. He argues that, after the British colonisation of large areas of Africa, the settlers' misguided and fundamentally ignorant agricultural policies disturbed this stable ecological balance and caused widespread epidemics that exposed millions of local labourers and their families to the ravages of this virulent disease.

Helge Kjekshus[2] describes the impact of colonisation in Tanzania from the 1890s as leading to 'ecological catastrophes' with the introduction of diseases such as rinderpest which caused widespread devastation to domestic and wild animals throughout that country and the wider region. He, too, draws attention to the environmental damage caused to pastoral systems and old pastoral lifestyles by Europeans' thoughtless clearances of forests.

Pratik Chakrabarti[3] describes the economic promises of so-called constructive imperialism' as 'no more than presumption' and concludes that the reality for sub-Saharan Africa might better be described as an 'Imperial apocalypse'.

Based on such critical evidence, it is now clear that Tropical Medicine was, initially at least, far more a vehicle and excuse for expanding imperialist colonisation than anything to do with local people's health. Its prime beneficiaries were, overwhelmingly, the settlers rather than the citizens of the colonies.

Much of what passed for medical services in the developing world in this period, with the honourable exception of missionary medicine, was also an inferior imitation of the hospital-dominated service that characterised most Western health services in the same period. Mission hospitals such as Tosamaganga in Southern Tanzania and Mengo in Kampala, Uganda, were much more progressive, built to serve local communities, and still do so today.

In the new discipline of Tropical Medicine, the intended beneficiaries were primarily European settlers. As part of their missions to bring the benefits of the West to Africa after the decisions taken at the Berlin conference in 1885, the three leading European nations, Britain, France and Germany, each established, albeit in different forms, but not coincidentally, Schools of Tropical Medicine to support their work in the African countries they had colonised. The Schools struggled at first to develop clear goals or working methods, partly because of a lack of proper understanding of the conditions they were supposed to treat. In the late nineteenth century, there was no scientific knowledge about the distinction between bacteriology and parasitology in providing explanations for dealing with conditions like malaria or sleeping sickness. The emphasis given to the needs of settlers was demonstrated very clearly, for example, in hospital provision in every colony, far more beds were always available for settlers than for local people. For example, Germany provided hospital care disproportionately for its soldiers in Tanganyika during its colonial rule before WW1. There was a disparity of more than 20 to 1 – in the number of hospital beds provided for soldiers and for African citizens in the capital, Dar es Salaam.

In Ibadan in Northern Nigeria before WW2, about 500 Europeans were served by 11 beds in a modern hospital. There were 34 beds for the half-million Nigerians. Across Nigeria as a whole, there were about 4000 Europeans served by 12 hospitals., The African population of 40 million had access to 52 hospitals. That equates to 1/200th of the level of service available to settlers.

This discrepancy started to change once it was realised that if the colonialists wanted to profit more from their colonies, they might need to focus on meeting their subjects' health needs.

Joseph Chamberlain, the British Colonial Secretary, suggested that better health care for local workers, as distinct from settlers, would be key to improved profitability. Before then, colonialists had been prepared to work their labourers to death, as seen in the Congo's depopulation during King Leopold and Lord Lever's regimes. Although Chamberlain's ideas were seemingly more humane, the evidence from various sources suggests that despite these efforts, other policies – such as the land clearances and inappropriate agricultural schemes which the colonists pursued – only served to introduce and spread new and existing diseases and epidemics and allow family poverty levels and malnutrition to increase. The colonialists had not even learned from the lessons of their own countries where previously endemic diseases such as malaria, cholera, and leprosy had been controlled or eliminated. This had been achieved primarily by making environmental improvements, such as secured food supplies, clean water, and better sanitation and housing. The view that the tropics were more inherently unhealthy was mistaken. This realisation was one of the factors that led the WHO to propose in 1978 that better local health services should be the objective in every country.[4]

Further evidence about the continued failings of Tropical Medicine to adequately address child malnutrition can still be seen in the fifth and most recent, Fifth edition (2021) of the well-known *Oxford Handbook of Tropical Medicine*.[5] In this guide for clinicians, there is scant recognition of the widespread problem of child malnutrition and just a single paragraph about its prevention, despite it being far and away the primary cause of early child deaths. Unlike earlier editions, there is no reference to the vital joint WHO/UNICEF document *Integrated Management of Childhood Illness*, which should be required reading for all clinicians working in the tropics. However, chapter after chapter in the Handbook describes the treatment of individual conditions such as renal disorders or dermatology, which are far less widespread than malnutrition. This disappointing guide may explain why hospital doctors in SSA appear to take so little interest in Stunting. It is as if doctors specialising in Tropical Medicine today are still locked into a time warp, unaware of the overriding importance of the broader social and economic environment in poorer countries or ignorant of the significance of preventative public health.

Turning again to the particular problems of child malnutrition, the story is yet again one of Western medical incompetence described in what has become known as *The True Fiasco: The treatment and Prevention of Severe Acute Malnutrition in Uganda* (Giles-Vernick and Jr, 2013).

Research into child malnutrition in Africa has had a seriously chequered history. Scientists and doctors were seriously at odds with each other and often failed to identify its different manifestations until the end of the 20th century. A breakthrough in understanding malnutrition came from Dr Cicely Williams,[6] and her remarkable and impressive career. She was one of the first women paediatricians in the early 20th century. As a Woman Medical Officer, she was paid at a lower rate than male doctors within the Colonial Medical Service. In her first post, in Ghana, she was caught up in a fierce debate about acute child malnutrition, often diagnosed as pellagra. She strongly disagreed with this and argued that it was a very different condition, known locally in Ghana as 'kwashiorkor'. It took Dr Williams to bring determined and persistent clarity to the confusion that had existed at that time. She boldly argued that: K*washiorkor was a disease caused mainly through a lack of knowledge and information*. Because of this, she was transferred 'in disgrace' to Malaya. There, she was instrumental in confronting the disgraceful practice of Nestle in employing female sales staff dressed as nurses to persuade mothers that their sweetened condensed milk was a preferable replacement for breast milk. She spoke out against this practice, calling it *Tantamount to Murder*, much to her male colleagues' annoyance.

After the invasion of Malaysia by the Japanese in December 1941, she was sent to Changi, the infamous prison where she was severely mistreated. This didn't prevent her from helping fellow women prisoners, some of whom had been pregnant and gave birth in that camp. After her return to England, she wrote a report on this, in which she noted: *20 babies were born, 20 babies were breastfed, and 20 babies survived. You can't do better than that!*

She later became the first Head of the new Maternal and Child Health Division of the World Health Organisation based in Geneva. Subsequently, she oversaw a survey to look at kwashiorkor in ten countries in sub-Saharan

Africa. This study described the condition known as Wasting to be 'the most serious and widespread condition known to medical or nutritional science.' Throughout her remarkable career, and unlike most other doctors of her time, she clearly saw the importance of combining preventative and curative medicine. Few people could have contributed more substantially to child health and nutrition than her.[7]

One obstacle preventing researchers from getting a clear picture of the types of malnutrition has been an obsession with a search for treatments and cures to neglect conditions where cures are not likely or possible. Their hypotheses led them right up to the mid-1950s to use blatantly cruel investigation methods, which alarmed parents so much that many removed their children from the hospital in question. One technique, for example, involved tiny children being harnessed, after first being bled, to a wooden structure called a balance bed for up to four days to collect samples of their urine and faeces for analysis. It was an object lesson in how even relatively recent public health programmes were poorly and cruelly managed and where parents' and communities' views were foolishly ignored (Clegg & Dean, 1960).[8]

Although, in the end, nutritional treatments were identified that provided effective remedies for severe acute malnutrition, nothing remotely similar was done to look at those chronically malnourished children, i.e. Stunted. Western-trained doctors were obsessed with treatment and cures and oblivious to the possibility that some conditions were not caused by infection or parasites. Thus, they could not see Prevention as a more fruitful avenue to pursue. The concept of public health and what are termed 'non-pharmaceutical interventions' are, of course, familiar to modern doctors. However, that does not seem to have been the case for many decades, especially in the colonies. This failure appears to have been a prime cause of the long-term institutional neglect of Stunting.

Even today, and as I can bear direct witness, some senior and respected doctors working in teaching hospitals in Uganda are still not recognising or dealing with the needs of chronically malnourished children who are not amenable to 'treatments'. When I asked consultant paediatricians at a major hospital in Uganda how they dealt with children suffering from Stunting, I was told that they didn't and that the only malnourished children they worked with on the wards were those suffering from Severe Acute Malnutrition.

It seems that they are so wedded to the importance of 'cure' that they do not seem to grasp the idea that the answer for these children lies outside their hospitals in the form of environmental improvements needing to be made in the homes and communities where children are born and spend their early lives. Not all doctors take this view, but those who think more widely about working with malnourished children seem to be a small minority. This is staggering when it is so clear now that Stunting is known to be the most significant contributory cause of infant deaths, even though its prevention lies with communities rather than hospitals.

Far too much emphasis is still placed on clinical treatments and cures when a multi-agency community-based prevention policy is more effective and would benefit many more children. A review by Kristina Reinhardt and Jessica Fanzo[11] helpfully describes the need for physicians to understand the need to work with other agencies if stunting is to be reduced and prevented. This isn't an approach familiar to many clinically trained and focused doctors. However, it is essential that doctors in sub-Saharan Africa recognise this and that it becomes part of their daily practice.

Across southern Africa, and for decades, the practice of curative medicine through the agency of 'Tropical Medicine ' has much to answer for in neglecting preventive health services. This shortsightedness has contributed very significantly to the ongoing neglect of Stunting and its lethal impact on millions of children.

One can only guess what might have been achieved over those years if Tropical Medicine and its practitioners had looked more carefully at their child patients' social and economic environments instead of being blind to what now seems so obvious and repeating the same ill-informed mistakes made by their fellow colonialists.

Partly to blame for this in East Africa lies in how the British took a highly questionable route to provide clinically focused health care. As John Iliffe has comprehensively illustrated in his study 'East African Doctors',[12] the chosen path was to copy the traditional way in which doctors were trained in Britain by requiring medical students to undertake extended training both in college/University and in hospital wards under the close supervision of experienced consultants. The objective was to produce very well-trained and high-status hospital-based doctors whose qualifications would be internationally recognised rather than considering alternative ways of meeting the needs of the citizens of these predominantly rural countries. It successfully achieved a cadre of very able, politically aware, independently minded professionals who turned out to be thorns in the side of African governments after independence in the 1960s. It may be thought that this was no mean achievement. However, it is much more debatable whether this approach was advantageous to most families and their children. Equipped with their desirable and portable qualifications, many newly qualified African doctors found it more beneficial to seek employment abroad, a trend that has continued to the present day. Yet others preferred to move into private practice because of the higher salaries there. And many chose to work in the more convenient jobs available in capital city hospitals, such as those in Nairobi, Kampala and Dar es Salaam. Together, these movements left significant gaps in the health services available to most people who lived in rural communities outside larger cities. Over the following decades, it became clear that this was a significant deficit. Other ways of meeting the health needs of citizens who didn't live in cities needed to be considered – but weren't.

Writing about health care in Tanzania, one of the world's poorest countries, Malcolm Segall[13] wrote that prevention, not treatment, was the most effective way of using minimal resources:

Prevention (with basic curative services) can improve the health of the mass of people within the very tight health budget. It is cheap; it can be effective. It alone can break the vicious circle of disease – treatment- recurrence- disease.

He gives these two impressive examples:

1. *A man has hookworm anaemia (common in Tanzania). He has been ill for years, and has to stop work altogether. He is admitted to hospital. He needs laboratory tests, skilled medical and nursing attention, drug treatment and a blood transfusion. After a time, he improves, and eventually, he goes back to work. At home, he catches hookworm again: the whole process is repeated. None of this would have happened if his village had used pit latrines.*
2. *A child has kwashiorkor: he develops diarrhoea, pneumonia, ear infection and septic skin. He already has worms and anaemia. He develops heart failure. He needs prolonged hospital care, highly skilled attention and much expensive treatment. Even then, he might die. None of this would have happened if his mother had known what to feed him.'*

These examples starkly show how Western colonial powers failed to identify the overall health care needs of the populations over whom they held influence and responsibility. They demonstrate the high-minded but mistaken belief that services and policies that had worked back in Europe would inevitably be suitable for Africa. The grossly erroneous assumption of the colonial powers was that the tropics were perennially ridden with disease and infection that needed their intervention to create the conditions for profitable activities that would benefit them.

The colonisers' dogmatic belief in African 'otherness,' and inferiority prevented them from seeing malnourishment for what it clearly was. Instead, scientists and administrators preferred to pursue wilder ideas, including protein deficiency or population growth as the chief causes of hunger. In doing this, as their tropical health counterparts had done, nutritionists seemed unable to distance themselves from the colonial mission and failed to see Africans as fellow human beings.

Given the evidence of significantly different levels of health care provision in the colonial era, it is clear that in Tropical Medicine, African children's health was never given anything close to the same priority as settlers' children. Perhaps this was because African children's health was unrelated to the profits being made in the colonies, They were not, it appears, seen as deserving the same medical care standards as the colonisers' children. Another highly plausible explanation for this is that racial prejudice was just as common within medical practice in the tropics as it was more generally amongst Europeans working in Africa.

The idea also seemed to exist that medicine in 'the tropics' was inherently 'foreign' and not amenable to the same scientific discipline that had started to inform and guide the profession's development in Europe during the twentieth century. The early practitioners of Tropical Medicine repeated the mistakes of their early Victorian urban counterparts in seeing disease as part of some mysterious 'miasma' rather than simply as manifestations of infections or the consequences of adverse environmental factors such as contaminated water or inadequate sanitation.

Yet again, it is clear that opportunities have been scandalously missed to meet the manifest needs of children in sub-Saharan Africa. Much of the blame for that rests on the shoulders of colonisers and doctors who were blinkered in their thinking about Africa. They came to the continent full of prejudices about the continent and were sure that they knew how to respond to the diseases they found. Unfortunately, their ideas of 'tropical' diseases bore no relation to the actuality of disease even as it was understood at that time, and their 'remedies' frequently turned out to be positively harmful both to humans and animals.

The fact that Schools of Tropical Medicine were established about the same time in Britain, Germany, Portugal, Netherlands, and Belgium and not long after the Scramble for Africa conference of 1897 speaks volumes about their true purpose, regardless of the title given to their existence and more recent and comfortable narratives as to the historical significance of this speciality. Doctors generally acted very similarly to settlers and Empire builders in this respect.

Notes and Guide to Further Reading

Global Health in Africa – historical perspectives on Disease 'Control (2013) Tamara Giles-Vernick and James L.A. Webb.
This is a bold and lively exploration of doctors' mistakes during different historical eras in Africa when far too little attention was given to socio-economic issues.

Barefoot Doctors and Western Medicine in China (2012) Xiaoping Fang
This relatively recent book distances itself from other somewhat nostalgic accounts of barefoot medicine, a term used to describe the fairly simple form of community first aid widespread in China before President Mao's Cultural Revolution. It is an intriguing account of how this precursor of modern biomedicine provided the foundation for effective nationwide primary health care there.

However, in many countries across SSA, it was mistakenly thought that Western and hospital-based medicine was the best way to deal with ill health. This crucial failure to invest in Africa's community health services has been one of the fundamental causes of child health and development neglect. The consequences of this fundamental mistake are very much with us today.

Medicine and Empire 1600-1960, Pratik Chakrabarti, op. cit.
Dr Chakrabarti explains that his account was written to 'bridge the divide between social and biomedical sciences to improve the delivery of global health services', a task still far from completed across the continent, especially

regarding child health and nutrition. This is an invaluable description and frank analysis of how so-called 'tropical medicine' became inseparably linked with imperialism's growth. It highlights how this forced marriage failed to ensure that decent and universal health care services were made available in sub-Saharan Africa and Asia. It is especially relevant in light of global pandemics such as Covid 19. It is particularly useful in explaining why so many child deaths were, and still are, attributable to unattended social and environmental issues.

Chapter 7

The missed opportunity; the World Bank's failure to develop primary health care in Africa, and the long-term price of that paid by Africa's children

During the Second World War and in the years after, there was great interest across the world in the idea of social medicine and in how medicine could be placed within a much broader framework of services which, together, could contribute to the social and economic reconstruction of a world that had been so damaged by war. Lord Beveridge's work on this in the UK, entitled 'Social Insurance and Allied Services', led to the setting up in 1947 of the National Health Service alongside a broader set of public services, including education and employment.

At the international level and following the Bretton Woods, New Hampshire, Conference of 1942, several international organisations, including the United Nations, the World Bank, and the World Health Organisation, were established. This latter development could be said to have been anticipated by the Rockefeller Foundation, which had created an International Health Commission as early as 1913, mainly to deal with the problems that hookworm had posed to labour productivity in tropical countries around the globe. Although Rockefeller may not have been entirely motivated by increasing his own wealth, it is clear that the Foundation's predominant purpose in the developing world was always to enhance the profits of companies and colonial governments. The Foundation continued to be a hugely influential organisation even after WW2. When the World Health Organisation had, in theory, replaced its role, it struggled at first to develop a distinctive voice in framing ideas about global Health and primary health care.

However, this changed significantly with the appointment in 1973 of its third Director-General, Dr Halfdan Mahler, a hugely impressive and visionary

Dr Halfdan Mahler Director – General WHO 1977-1988

man who had worked for the Rockefeller Foundation on campaigns to tackle tuberculosis in India.

Shortly after his arrival as the incoming Director-General, the WHO commenced a study to assess the work of many innovative community health programmes worldwide. This was done to explore a vision of health far more comprehensive than the traditional medical practice model. The innovators of these projects had been fired by the more inclusive concepts of community and social medicine. One influential and international post-war grouping to develop these grounds breaking and radical ideas after WW2 drew on Article 25 of the United Nations Universal Declaration of Human Rights: *Everyone has the right to a standard of living adequate for the health and wellbeing of themselves and their families, including food, clothing, housing, and medical care and necessary social services.*[1]

Drawing on this and the promising outcomes of the international fieldwork, he declared: *The potentialities are great if the WHO can become the spearhead for a movement for the social and economic betterment of the underdeveloped counties while also serving as the channel for the exchange of ideas on health administration across all countries.*

This radical and forward-thinking definition of 'public health' went way beyond the traditional view of that speciality and included a list of services that contribute to health, including social welfare, social security, environmental sanitation, food production and distribution, and education.

Paradoxically, it was the Rockefeller Foundation that had first been interested in this different way of thinking about public health. It had even sponsored some earlier work to look at ideas such as the rural community health programmes such as 'the barefoot doctor' concept developed in China as far back as the 1930s. At a relatively low cost, this approach provided adequate health care services, especially in rural areas facing economic and environmental challenges not dissimilar to those in many parts of Africa and where some integration with aspects of traditional medicine was felt necessary. Several advisers working for the Rockefeller Foundation were sympathetic to China's changes, which linked primary health care improvements to the more extensive rural reconstruction efforts adopted by the incoming Chinese government's leadership.

But, ironically, and given its own record of interest and involvement in these pioneering developments, the Rockefeller Foundation played a prominent role in the World Bank's rejection in the early 1980s of the relatively similar proposals that WHO had put forward. One explanation for this about-turn in thinking this lay in the American fear, if not paranoia, of communism, which reared its head in Africa's independence movements during the '70s and '80s. This was shown most clearly when the USA intervened in the affairs of several emerging new governments in sub-Saharan Africa, most infamously in Congo, where, as mentioned earlier, the elected President, Patrice Lumumba, was assassinated by groups now widely thought to have been supported by the CIA because of his left-leaning policies. After WW2 and the African Independence movements, the USA's involvement in Africa didn't receive the same critical attention as European colonialism. The Americans, distasteful of colonisation and having experienced it themselves at the British hands, did not wish to become latter-day colonisers. However, as will become clear later, they were just as attracted by the prospects of making profits from Africa, albeit by different means.

Even today, many seemingly reasonable and fair-minded Americans show a deep antipathy towards public health and 'Obamacare', which is seen as akin to communism. So embedded in modern Britain as a foundation stone of civilised life, the National Health Service is widely there today with suspicion. Just why that should be is a mystery but must stem partly from the Cold War period when even socialism, let alone communism, was seen as alien concepts and absolutely at odds with 'American values'.

The feedback from the WHO's 1975 review of community health

programmes was published as *Health by the People*.[2] It included highly encouraging reports, including those about village health teams working in Niger, how basic health needs were being adequately met in rural Tanzania, and about effective and practical projects from countries as disparate as Venezuela, Iran, China, Guatemala, and Cuba.

The vital and innovative concept that emerged from the studies was that of 'community medicine', described as a realistic, practical, and unsophisticated approach to meeting people's basic needs and demands, especially in remote and isolated regions. But no one model applied everywhere, and each community seemed to find its particular way of seeing that children were adequately fed without bureaucratic uniformity in how this was achieved. The report ends with this extraordinarily moving account of a meeting with a health assistant in a project in Costa Rica who asked about records on births and deaths and became embarrassed when asked about the deaths of children under one year of age.

The report's author, Dr Kenneth Newell, one of the Directors of WHO, movingly concluded: *This humble, successful health worker was incredulous that his efforts had brought about so dramatic an improvement.* He said: *'Children did die in my first year here – but none have died in the second year. I have checked and cross-checked with the families, but all the children are still alive. I cannot account for it.*

One of the headline findings from this study was that the most successful projects almost always used 'health care workers', which challenged the traditional roles of both doctors and nurses. Health care workers were seen in all the schemes as the key to success because they were accepted by the communities and could deal with local problems better than anyone had done before and because – above all – they were there.

As a direct consequence of these and several other encouraging pilots and evaluations, WHO and UNICEF together decided to adopt an action programme to develop community-based primary health care along similar lines in all developing countries, particularly those with inadequately provided health care services such as in rural and remote areas or slums or where there were nomadic populations. It was also recommended that primary health care should be integrated into an overall pattern of community services that included nutrition, education, the provision of clean water and improved sanitation, and better transport and communication, all of which had a contribution to make towards the improvement of people's health and wellbeing.

The responsibility for taking this groundbreaking thinking forward fell to Dr Mahler, the WHO's charismatic Director-General, who recognised that the time was right for radical change, significantly when the global political climate was also changing as African nations pressed the case for their independence.

Dr Mahler used the World Health Assembly meeting in 1976 to boldly promote 'Health for All by the Year 2000' with this target as a clarion call for change. He said: *Many social evolutions and revolutions had taken place because social structures were crumbling. There are also signs*, he added, *that public health's scientific and technical structures are crumbling.*

In taking this step, he laid the foundation for a highly significant international conference set to take place two years later. It was a turning point in the debate about how global primary health care would be fashioned over the following decades. Marius Cueto has meticulously documented this.[3]

The conference, attended by over 3000 delegates from 134 countries, including the USA and 67 international organisations, was held in Alma Ata, a city in the Soviet Republic of Kazakhstan. In attendance were representatives from the United Nations, the Food and Agriculture Organisation, the Red Cross, and, remarkably. from several political organisations, including the Palestine Liberation Organisation and SWAPO, the revolutionary group that recently helped achieve Namibia's independence. Many delegates were senior managers and officials in health ministries who were significantly influential in their countries.

Mahler was uncompromisingly outspoken and courageous from the outset and asked delegates if they were prepared to commit their governments and agencies to radical change to give priority to making a reality of primary health care and to be prepared to fight off the inevitable challenges from professional groups and from those who questioned the affordability and achievability of global primary health care.

These challenges had been carefully discussed in preliminary regional meetings organised by WHO months before the conference. Countries were forewarned about the inevitability of counterarguments, especially those of affordability and priority.

Also anticipated was a backlash from elite groups such as city hospital-based doctors and others unready to cede their social status to less well-trained health care workers. Significantly, although not always recognised, Mahler had emphasised that primary health care was not going to be a 'one size fits all' idea but rather a new way of understanding and working within an integrated system of health and social care and part of the social and economic changes that were needed in developing countries over the long term. He stated that health should be a vital instrument for development, not a by-product of economic progress. This remarkably prescient view turned out to be, as will be seen, a crucially significant and strategic statement, given the entirely different perspectives that were to be expressed in later decades by the World Bank and others.

The conference, a milestone event in twentieth-century thinking about health and its place in the developing world, ended in Sept 1978 with a Declaration urging governments to commit to a community-based model of primary health care to be achieved by 2000 as Dr Mahler had hoped – in short, the attainment of 'Health for All' around the globe.

The Declaration was unanimously supported by all countries, including the United States – an important outcome given the sheer diversity of interests involved – and one that held out enormous promise for the future of children's health and nutrition across the globe.

The highlight of the conference described later by Dr Mahler as a 'sacred moment' involved a young African physician who stood up at the end of the meeting and read out the most critical wording of the Declaration, which had been unanimously agreed, as here:

The International Conference on Primary Health Care, meeting in Alma-Ata this 12th of September in 1978, expressing the need for urgent action by all governments, all health and development workers, and the world community to protect and promote the health of all the people of the world, now makes the following Declaration, part of which is set out below because of its great importance as the framework of ideas which still represents the most coherent and integrated statement ever made about what primary health care should entail.

I

The Conference strongly reaffirms that health, which is a state of complete physical, mental and social wellbeing, and not merely the absence of disease or infirmity, is a fundamental human right and that the attainment of the highest possible level of health is the most important worldwide social goal whose realisation requires the action of many other social and economic sectors in addition to the health sector.

II

The existing gross inequality in the people's health status, particularly between developed and developing countries and within countries, is politically, socially, and economically unacceptable and, therefore, of common concern.

III

Based on a New International Economic Order, economic and social development is of basic importance to the fullest attainment of health for all and the reduction of the gap between the health status of the developing and developed countries. The promotion and protection of the health of the people are essential to sustained economic and social development and contribute to a better quality of life and to world peace.

IV

The people have the right and duty to participate individually and collectively in the planning and implementation of their health care.

This declaration represented a pivotal and critical moment in developing thinking and policy about global health, especially primary health care in developing countries. Had it been used as the basis for action, the problems of childhood mortality and malnutrition that had been so problematic across the Third World could have been resolved or made much less severe.

But the understandable euphoria that WHO and its supporters must have felt was, regrettably, short-lived. What happened is both sobering and disappointing in the extreme. Although the USA delegates had voted unanimously in support of the Alma Ata Declaration, concerns soon surfaced within the World Bank, and the Rockefeller and Ford Foundations regarding the financial viability of recommendations agreed at the international conference. A group of influential scientists, doctors, politicians, and heads of some voluntary agencies and national foundations also seem to have been alarmed at what they chose to think were the Declaration's extravagant and unrealistic consequences. Although Mahler had clearly talked about a 'direction of travel' rather than a specific destination, its principal detractors saw it very differently. Instead of international agencies working together to plan a way forward based on the Declaration, as might have been expected, these few but very influential organisations were not persuaded and decided to look at other and cheaper alternatives, the most significant of these being called Selective Primary Health Care (PHC). Instead of the 'horizontal' and global development of Primary Health Care as Mahler had suggested, this involved a model involving 'vertical', cheaper and more measurable interventions focusing on just a few arbitrarily pre-selected conditions, including malaria, measles and diarrhoea.

This much more cautious change of thinking seems to have been triggered partly by the World Bank's President Robert McNamara, who had stated, timidly, in the Bank's annual report in 1978 that: *'Even if the projected and optimistic growth rates in the developing world are achieved, some 600 million individuals at the end of the century will remain trapped in absolute poverty. Absolute poverty is a condition of life characterised by malnutrition, illiteracy, disease, and low life expectation beneath any reasonable definition of human decency.'*[4]

Although this hand-wringing is touching, it is an enormous pity that McNamara seems not to have listened to what Dr Mahler and his team were saying at Alma Ata about global health's potential to help with development rather than waiting for it help to come from economic change.

A management consultant by training, Robert McNamara had served as America's discredited Secretary of Defence during the Vietnam War. Although judging from his writings to be a well-intentioned man, it is not surprising, given his background as a work-study expert, that he supported the much cheaper option for the future of primary health care even though this was in complete contradiction to what had been decided at Alma Ata as a consequence of the visionary thinking and field research of Mahler and WHO, as well as those many supporters across the world for a much more comprehensive approach to health care.

It seems clear now that McNamara's limited imagination and timidity killed off the visionary thinking of Mahler and the WHO, just as it failed him in his capacity as American Secretary of Defence. Given America's schizophrenic past concerning slavery and its more recent attitude to African independence movements, racial prejudice is also very likely to have played a part. Why would a country that so severely mistreated its own black citizens want to prioritise investing in a model of health care provision to benefit poorer countries, including those in sub-Saharan Africa?

Within a year, a highly selective conference was convened to discuss these reservations at the Rockefeller Foundation's international conference centre at Bellagio in Italy, involving the Ford and Rockefeller Foundations, The World

Bank, UNICEF, and compliant academics from medical schools in Harvard and Boston. No representatives were present or even invited from WHO or Europe, or even more significantly, from any countries or experts from the developing world.

Papers to endorse a much more cautious approach were submitted by David Bell from the Ford Foundation, Julia A. Walsh from Harvard, and Kenneth S. Warren from Brigham Young hospital, Boston – who had examined what was called the Selective Primary Health Care model and recommended it as being more achievable and cost-effective than the more open-ended and generic Primary Health Care model which WHO had supported.[5] The assumptions made by these researchers were highly questionable. For example, they dismissed far too readily the potential that environmental changes can have on what they termed 'protean' diseases such as cholera. They repeated the same mistakes made by other expatriate doctors decades earlier in Africa, where treatment was always considered more effective than prevention.

Their analysis helped provide a veneer of scientific respectability to help American business people and financiers reject the remarkable vision and ambition of the World Health Organisation. This, it needs to be remembered, had been solidly grounded in carefully evaluated trials worldwide of a new way of delivering better health care. The academics asked, disingenuously, *'How in an age of diminishing resources can we best secure the Health and wellbeing of those trapped at the bottom of the scale long before 2000?'* Just what was meant by their phrase 'diminishing resources' was not elaborated, although it now sounds like weasel words chosen to appeal to McNamara and the businessmen whose interests lay elsewhere.

David Bell, the Medical Director at the Ford Foundation,[6] praised WHO's good intentions but predictably cautioned about the lack of reliable data informing WHO's proposals and costings. He said, in effect, that at a time of 'scarce resources', they might not be affordable and that a more cautious approach based on steady improvements in health care in developing countries might be a wiser course. Again, his affiliations and loyalties speak for themselves.

When the HIV/AIDS epidemic, some decades later, seemed to threaten American lives and security, no such questions of affordability arose, and the $200 plus billion spent on combatting this condition was more generous than what it would have cost to make substantial improvements in primary health care globally.

The reaction from the developing world to the devastating about-turn has been fiercely critical. Some voices spoke of the West having converted 'primary' into 'primitive'. Many were disappointed that community-based social medicine's vision was replaced by the top-down 'We Know Best' strategy, which the United States subsequently imposed. It is hard not to think that this entire process of 'review' was nothing more than a cover to justify the American establishment's lack of interest in and concern for the developing world, especially when it might have involved significant expenditure and threatened their commercial priorities.

Further humiliation for WHO came when UNICEF, of all organisations, decided to put its considerable weight behind the 'Selective' model despite having previously supported the community-led Global health care concept. Under the leadership of their hugely ambitious Director James Grant, UNICEF embarked on a campaign, cynically described as a 'Children's Revolution,' to commit to a programme of vaccinations focussed on a few conditions which were known to be dangerous for children, as had been recommended to the Bellagio conference, but which fell far short of the kind of fundamental and more sustainable shift to social and preventive medicine which had been so positively endorsed at Alma Ata.

After Bellagio and UNICEF's change of heart and self-serving betrayal, the WHO was effectively side-lined as the prime influencer of opinion about global health. After it changed its view, UNICEF took centre stage as the saver of children's lives, despite having argued previously and alongside Dr Mahler at WHO about the importance of prevention and community-based primary health care. Paul Farmer has roundly condemned this episode as representing 'Wealth Over Health.'

This enormously disappointing and shameful saga must be seen against China's substantial body of evidence about a significant trial of community-based and simplified medicine. This demonstrated that this health care approach could be highly effective. Numerous reports on the effectiveness of the 'barefoot doctor' system practiced for over 50 years in China, as well as in the more recent work led by UNICEF itself involving the use of local health assistants in different countries, have shown them to make a measurable difference to the health and wellbeing of people in local communities (UNICEF, 2013).[7]

This outcome of the debate between Primary Health Care and Selective Primary Health Care was a massive blow for those who had wished for significant improvements in the way in which health care was seen and delivered in the Third World and was a hugely retrograde step in the drive to tackle child malnutrition using multi-agency integrated work so very far removed from the short term disease-specific approach implicit in SPHC.

In the years after the rejection of Primary Health Care by the World Bank, there has been further analysis of the impact of that decision and discussion about the real motivation underlying the American decision. On this second point, American academic Nicholas King[8] has drawn attention to the very different emphasis placed by the United States when seeing 'emergent diseases' in developing countries as potential threats to its security and commercial interests. Previously such conditions were felt to be mainly of concern to these poor foreign countries and contained within their boundaries. However, this changed when diseases such as Ebola and HIV/Aids began to be seen as serious threats to American trade and security and marked a change in thinking and policy. Some of that thinking was geared, chillingly, to looking for ways American companies might be able to profit from opportunities to *transform human suffering into and exchanged as a commodity.*' As it was put by Kassalow:[9] *'This post-colonial thinking had the potential for world health improvements to strengthen the global system, which, in turn, benefits the United States as the dominant power and leading supporter of that system'*. Less financially calculatingly than this have been several analyses of the actual effectiveness of SPHC compared with what PHC itself might have achieved. One such review, carried out by a team of American epidemiologists led by Leslie Magnussen[10] concluded: *'Primary health care was declared the model for global health policy at a 1978 meeting of health ministers and experts from around the world… It was considered too idealistic and expensive and replaced with a disease-focused, selective model. After several years of investment in vertical interventions, preventable diseases remain a major challenge for developing countries. The selective model has not responded adequately to the interrelationship between health and socioeconomic development, and a rethinking of global health policy is urgently needed.'*

Two Australian specialists, John Hall and Richard Taylor[11], writing in 2003 about the outcome of the decision in the early 1980s to scrap Primary Health Care, point to the widening gap between citizens' living standards and incomes in the prosperous north as compared with those experienced by those in developing countries. The underlying causes of poverty, ill-health, and inadequate education are not being addressed by neoliberalism, as clearly seen in the high rates of poverty and malnutrition still to be seen worldwide.

The *volte-face* made by UNICEF, the World Bank and American business interests effectively ended Dr Mahler's career and influence on global health thinking. It ruined the primacy of the World Health Organisation for more than a generation. Damaged by this defeat, WHO's subsequent profile was significantly reduced to a far less imposing or active presence on the international health scene.

It is worth considering why the USA firmly rejected such an essential idea as Primary Health Care. Some have suggested that it was an idea so radical as to be before its time. Others have blamed the WHO for not preparing its audience carefully enough and not clarifying that what was suggested was for a 'direction of travel' and an 'idea' instead of a highly detailed plan of action. Both must have been, to a degree, right, as the outcome was so decidedly negative. It is hard to agree with the first of these suggestions, given the unanimous support given to the Alma Ata Conference's proposals. More likely, Dr Mahler failed to recognise that even unanimous World Conference resolutions taken with professional delegates' support don't make the final decisions that countries, and in the case of the USA, its major companies, will wish to support politically and financially. (A very similar situation has arisen in the current Covid 19 pandemic. The USA, or at least its former President, Donald Trump, refused to listen to unequivocal and professional advice from the WHO about how a deadly virus should be contained.)

This unfortunate saga has been extraordinarily damaging for children in the developing world, especially in SSA. Numbers of children's lives were, no doubt, saved through the work of the selective, top-down approach to health care, which resulted from the decisions taken by the World Bank and the highly questionable collaboration of UNICEF. But the far more ambitious opportunity to tackle ill health and child malnutrition globally, as was proposed by Dr Mahler and the World Health Organisation, was tragically missed.

This lack of vision has had a massive and deadly impact on millions of children's lives and prospects and has set back for decades changes that only now are beginning to be made.

Another sad example of Western shortsightedness in thinking about how developing countries can best organise their health services can be seen in how, as a 'parting gift' to the newly independent government of Uganda, the British government chose to finance the building of a national showcase teaching/referral hospital at Mulago in Kampala. This increasingly dilapidated hospital still dominates Uganda's health service, as seen daily in the long queues of patients from far away and waiting to be seen within its poorly maintained wards. The odd and extraordinary exceptions to this picture of Mulago are the modern and well-equipped units recently built there and financed by American donors to specialise in their arbitrary and highly personal choice of diseases, including cancer and heart disease, rather than conditions that cry out for more attention in Africa. It would have been far preferable to focus on the more common conditions such as malnutrition or the more easily treatable but neglected tropical diseases such as Leishmaniasis and Chagas disease[12]. Better still would have been to invest in local clinics across the country, especially in the rural areas where levels of malnutrition are highest. One of the reasons such large hospitals were built in Africa is that most doctors preferred the convenience and the generous remuneration available to them in such surroundings. This kind of development followed from how modern medicine was introduced into Africa by Western doctors who could not see, any more than their farming predecessors had done decades earlier, that methods and priorities suitable for advanced nations in Europe might not be appropriate for an undeveloped and predominately rural Africa. They might have been wise to have followed the well-documented example of how China chose to deal with a similar problem in the 1930s of providing bottom-up health care in a mainly rural country and became institutionalised in the '60s after Mao Zedong saw it as an essential part of the Cultural Revolution.[13]

There is little evidence at present that African health service managers or practitioners have sufficient involvement with other agencies. This may change as the United Nations initiative Scaling up Malnutrition (SUN)[15] is more widely adopted. Still, until then, it continues to limit the work of those whose job is to protect children at risk of malnutrition or early death.

Worryingly, in SSA, many senior hospital-based clinicians ignore the fact that Stunting is responsible for killing many more child victims of malnutrition than Wasting. The obsession with the hospital-based treatment of acute malnutrition is blinding them to the predicament of millions of children being chronically malnourished in their local communities,

The laws to protect children from harm in most countries in SSA are, it has been shown, different from those in the UK and USA and do not include malnutrition and poverty as fundamental causes of neglect. Because these conditions are so common in SSA, legal protections for children are deficient. This deficiency may be why clinicians, such as social workers and doctors, have problems focusing on chronic malnutrition cases. See Bergeron.[16]

Another considerable obstacle to preventing doctors in SSA from paying attention to child malnutrition is how international donors have prioritised certain conditions. The most conspicuous example of this can be seen in the way that health services have been dominated by donors such as Bill and Melinda Gates and others whose wealth allows them to dictate the way that health and social services are delivered even when the evidence is that their ideas are at odds with the real needs of citizens. Some British donors, including Stagecoach, have, for example, been building orphanages when this is neither sensible nor necessary.

In 2007, the Global Fund[17] changed its responsibility for funding initiatives to tackle diseases such as HIV/AIDS and tuberculosis. The intention was to broaden its remit. However, it simply reinforced the World Bank's commitment to the selective health care model, which resulted from global discussions several decades earlier.

As a result of the Bank's obsession with certain conditions and treatments, very little time or money is available for African doctors to deal with Neglected Tropical Diseases (NTD) such as those mentioned earlier and others, including schistosomiasis and hookworm. These are not fatal conditions but cause great suffering to their victims, often poor villagers struggling to feed and care for their children. Rebecca Brosch op.cit. draws attention to the fact that these and several similar conditions could be cheaply and effectively treated – and sufferers would then be able to give more attention to their children's nutritional needs.

Other writers have reached similar conclusions about the impact of these decisions. A group of academics at MSF, Belgium, Canada, and the USA doubt whether adequate finance will ever become available to allow developing nations to develop local health services.

In recent years, the West's prioritisation of 'vertical ' interventions has been given even greater emphasis by a powerful and unholy combination of American pharmaceutical companies and wealthy Foundations, all strongly supported by the World Bank, keen to promote neoliberal policies. Their efforts have led to the medicalisation and commercialisation of health and favoured decision-making outside Africa.

This is another significantly overlooked instance of how Western and mainly American medical/political/ commercial priorities have been allowed to override the interests of African families and children. It explains why so many impoverished and chronically ill parents are not well enough to nurture their children adequately. It has driven another nail into whether global Primary Health Care (PHC), which had been the WHO's ambition decades earlier, could ever be achieved.

This 'magic bullet' approach, favoured by the Gates Foundation and the World Bank to deal with diseases by hi-tech, 'vertical' and primarily external interventions, has significantly weakened the continent's ability to develop local health care services. If there had been a more local and community-based structure for health services, it would have dealt much better with many illnesses and prevented infection and disease by prioritising improving hygiene standards.

Margaret Chan, a successor Director-General of the WHO, has made a similar point. She has described the over-dependence on vaccines, for Ebola, as failing to address conditions that generated the epidemic in the first place, leading eventually to the next global epidemic. She concludes: *'There is no replacement for robust and good, resilient health systems with the capability for surveillance.'*[18] Sadly, her comments are just as relevant today as when they were written more than a decade ago.

The current and severe impact of Covid 19 in Africa has again exposed the region's lack of local health service structures. A WHO report in May 2021[19] states that health facilities and personnel crucial for critically ill Covid 19 patients *'were grossly inadequate in many African countries.'* It found that most had less than one intensive care unit bed per 100.000 population, and only one-third had mechanical ventilators. In comparison, rich countries such as Germany have more than 25 ICU beds per 100,000 people.

There continues to be an over-reliance on large city-based hospitals in most countries and a corresponding shortage of local health centres, which could have offered a more effective response to this crisis.

Many writers are making the same point. For example, Paul Farmer at Harvard[20] has been eloquently arguing for reshaping global health provision to more effectively meet the needs of more impoverished communities such as those in Africa and South Asia. A former Chief Executive of the NHS, Nigel Crisp,[21] makes a similar case for fresh thinking and radical ideas if developing nations are to break out of this impasse.

It is not difficult to conclude that the entire episode of the rejection of the WHO's plans for global healthcare during the late 1970s, described in this chapter, was a massively missed opportunity to improve healthcare services for children and families both globally and significantly in SSA. In the decades between then and the more recent initiatives to tackle child malnutrition being led by the United Nations, of which more later, many millions of children's lives were lost. The blame for this can be placed predominantly on the narrow thinking of the World Bank and Foundations representing American businesses, as well as on the shameful selfishness of UNICEF, which seized an opportunity to establish itself as the world's leader in child welfare. Its emphasis on the vertical imposition of commercially successful drug treatments for a few preselected illnesses was the antithesis of the far wiser thinking of Dr Mahler and the World Health Organisation.

Notes and Guide to Further Reading
Health by the People, WHO (1975)
If one book conveys the importance of radical and relevant ideas about health care in the developing world, this is it. This is a convincing account of the various projects that were part of a joint WHO/ UNICEF global programme to examine community-based health care feasibility. Put together by Kenneth Newell, head of the Division of Strengthening of Health Services at WHO, it represents a radically different way of looking at how rural communities can work together to prevent maternal and child deaths. It includes reports from many countries, including Tanzania and Niger in Africa and other developing nations worldwide.

Another valuable commentary about Alma Ata's failure is in *Reimaging Global Heath* by Paul Farmer, a Harvard professor and a robust advocate for Primary Health Care until his recent death.

Dr Farmer has also written another extremely influential book *Pathologies of Power: Human Rights and the New War on the Poor*,[22,] a telling account of the increasing disparities in health and well-being within societies. It has been described as *'making a powerful case that our very humanity is threatened by our collective failure to end these abuses.'*

Farmer's analysis might well apply to the issues of child malnutrition and avoidable deaths, which are the subject of this book.

Marius Cueto has provided the most thorough description of the events covered in this Chapter. His paper, op cit, and related documents by Socrates Litsios[23] are sobering and desperately sad records of how an opportunity was missed to reshape the pattern of global health. They are testimonies to the overwhelming and pernicious influence of the United States and UNICEF on the lives of millions of children in the Third World. In both instances, self-interest prevailed. The USA showed little concern for solutions that did not benefit American companies or seemed communitarian and challenging to their cold war ideologies. UNICEF's position was driven simply by its then Director's boundless and crude ambition, who saw and grasped the opportunities that Selective Primary Health care would offer his organisation.

Neither the World Bank nor UNICEF has recognised that most of the problems besetting families in sub-Saharan Africa and other poor regions have been brought about by the vast inequalities that the West, including America, bestowed on them due to their outrageously greedy actions and policies over many years. By embarking on such timid responses as Selective Health Care, they were simply tinkering with a deadly situation that demanded a bold and progressive response, such as the model WHO had recommended.

More recently, British epidemiologist Michael Marmot[24] has drawn attention to the social and medical damage that structural inequality can cause in cities or nations. He gives the examples of Glasgow, UK and Baltimore, USA, notorious for poor health outcomes or crime. He argues that irrespective of the 'presenting problem', as seen in these cities, the causation – gross inequality – is the same. A similar argument extends to entire nations. Parents in Niger, Uganda, or Chad are no less concerned for their children's health than parents in San Francisco, Paris or London. The overriding and determining factor that leads to different health or educational outcomes for young children in their cities or nations is whether citizens are treated fairly. The evidence from over 7,000 studies for this radical and challenging conclusion is overwhelming for some. A UNICEF study, for example, showed that Western countries with the best outcomes for their children's well-being, such as Iceland, Sweden, and Germany, are where family poverty levels are low and where services to support families with young children are well developed. Conversely, countries with poor outcomes for children's well-being, such as the USA, Bulgaria and the United Kingdom, have high poverty levels. (UNICEF, 2013).

It doesn't take a second to translate this finding to the predicament of children in sub-Saharan Africa, where severe poverty is endemic in every country.

Of course, individual parents can make a difference for their children, but as Marmot concludes: *Population-wide determinants require social action. It doesn't help simply to say that it's up to the individual.*

In Africa, the appalling statistics for child health and well-being clearly show how the colonising countries and, more recently, the USA, have decided to place far more importance on taking resources from the continent rather than investing in better health care and education services for its children.

Many citizens' well-being counts for little to those in power whose priorities lie in maintaining their privilege and wealth creation. In most countries, and even in democracies, this has been a neglected topic. In recent years, several internationally renowned epidemiologists and economists, including Michael Marmot (op cit), Joseph Stiglitz[25] and Richard Wilkinson and Kate Pickett,[26] have written about the importance of equality in determining how effective governments have been in serving the interests of all their citizens.

Right-wing politicians and governments in the West should give this thinking more attention. It shows the significant differences in child mortality and life chances between wealthy countries such as the UK and the USA, where neoliberal policies have been dominant, and the more socially aware and egalitarian countries such as Scandinavia, the Netherlands and Germany. This picture is even more evident in the developing world, as explained next.

Chapter 8
Neoliberalism and its destructive impact on children's health and well-being in Africa

The Law of the Jungle, which Neoliberalism can be said to represent, and which creates and even celebrates inequality, has been shown to have strongly negative consequences for various nutritional, health, and educational problems worldwide.

Among Michael Marmot's international findings on the impact of inequality, neoliberal policies are shown to correlate directly with reduced life expectancy. The countries with the lowest life expectancy – Zambia, Swaziland, Angola, Zimbabwe, and Sierra Leone – are in sub-Saharan Africa. It is no coincidence that they also have the lowest average incomes globally.

After the enormous disruption caused by the Second World War, there was a period of almost half a century when global financial systems remained stable. This was significantly due to the British economist John Maynard Keynes who had anticipated and planned for the turmoil that would inevitably result from those years. His ideas were based on the need for balance between unfettered capitalism, which led to the Wall Street Crash in the 1920s, and full-scale state interventions that had led to communism. He believed that neither of these extremes was desirable and that 'mixed economies' represented a more sensible and appropriate model. In his thinking, public services such as education and health should rightly be the state's responsibility.

In the 1970s and 1980s, several economists, including Friedrich Hayek and Milton Friedman, challenged his ideas. They believed that 'the market ' should play a more significant part in economies' workings and that the private sector should be encouraged to play a more important role than it had. Their thinking was based mainly on concerns about the excesses that had taken place in the Soviet Union, where an all-powerful state had drastically curtailed individual freedom. This had been powerfully illustrated by the Russian author Alexander Solzhenitsyn, who described The Gulag's cruelties in which dissidents had been arrested and imprisoned without trial.

This radical thinking was developed by other economists, notably at Chicago University, as the basis for what became known as Neoliberalism, and which was, crucially, seen as attractive by President Reagan and Margaret Thatcher. Mrs Thatcher even questioned the importance of society, such as her belief in the overriding importance of individualism. In doing this, she completely failed to appreciate the significance of African countries' strong emphasis on community life and values. Reagan and Thatcher played a significant part in putting their version of these ideas into practice in the USA and Britain. It is fair to say that their enthusiastic approach bears little relationship to its authors' original concerns and ideas. However, it has become the official policy adopted by the World Bank and subsequently became the default concept for economic planning in Africa. The World Bank imposed it as a precondition for financial support on many governments. This extreme form of capitalistic thinking has been a failure, as evidenced most spectacularly by the financial crash of 2008 when many countries' economies were extraordinarily challenged and were forced to impose punitive levels of austerity and even when many leading banks and, most notably, Lehman Brothers in the USA, had to close.

Neoliberalism's benefits were stated by its proponents to 'trickle down' from wealthy companies and owners to everyone else, but there is no evidence that this has ever happened. It seems more likely that this was never its true intention. Reagan was never known to be concerned about the developing world and its children. Neither was Mrs Thatcher. Both could see that neoliberalism could offer an opportunity to make greater profits from post-independence Africa, and, thanks to the World Bank subsequently, this is precisely what has happened.

There are now many more millionaires both in the UK and the USA than ever before, but this has not helped tackle inequality or improve the lot of the most impoverished people in either country, whose livelihoods have become much more insecure with the advent of the 'gig' economy and by an increasingly and deliberately aggressive approach to 'welfare' and 'public services' being taken by right-wing governments. Britain compares unfavourably with most other countries in Europe in its commitment to equality and, in this respect, is more like the United States, where liberal ideas are anathema. Public health services are widely viewed as 'communistic', even though their private health services are costly, inefficient, and bureaucratic and fail to help millions of citizens.

Even in the West, there is much to suggest that Neoliberalism is a failure – witness the mismanagement and greed demonstrated at companies like Dupont and Boeing in the USA and Volkswagen in Germany, where, in each case, the relentless drive for profit at all costs has led their executives to behave deceitfully and caused harm to thousands of people in their pursuit of increased profits. The more recent evidence in the UK has been shown at the Grenfell Fire Inquiry has revealed that companies' dishonest behaviour in supplying cladding materials for high-rise flats in West London is the latest and most shocking example. Seventy-two people were killed when the cladding panels they provided caught fire. The manufacturers, Kingspan and Arconic, both lied about the safety of the materials they offered even though they admitted at the Inquiry knowing that they were highly combustible and entirely inappropriate for this purpose.

In the UK, the Conservative government has shown over a decade a readiness, based on Neoliberal ideas, to treat vulnerable groups such as refugees and low-income families with young children with little regard for their rights and dignity in its quest for political ends, primarily to drive down public services costs.

After the 2008 crash, the Conservative government deliberately chose to run down its investments in public services, including health care, services for under 5's, and public education, rather than increase taxation. This decision has played out rather spectacularly in recent times when the lack of readiness of the National Health Service has been so apparent in the UK's poor performance, when, for example, in comparison to Germany, in tackling the crisis brought about by the Covid-19 Pandemic.

During this global crisis, the resurgence of political support by the right for the National Health Service has been remarkable in the UK. This volte-face is all the more astonishing given that the same Conservative government had gone to enormous lengths after the financial crash to run down the service and privatise much of it. This sits very oddly with its present support and even an apparent enthusiasm for a publically-funded health service. In the event, the government has been keen to use untested partners in the private sector rather than look to the established expertise of local authorities and public health professionals in attempting to limit the spread of Covid or manage several Tests and Trace systems. These rash investments in the private sector have been demonstrably poor value for money. According to a just-published report by researchers at Oxford, they have not been accompanied by better health outcomes. It illustrates how far market-centred governments are prepared to pursue their beliefs. The World Bank's adoption of neoliberal ideas has been an even greater disaster for developing countries, particularly in SSA, where governments have been forced to cut public services for financial support.

Three Nigerian academics, Richard Ingwe, Chibuenze Okoro, and Felix Ojang[1] have summarised the impact of the neoliberal financial crash of 2007/8 on sub-Saharan African countries. They conclude:'*The global financial-economic crises of 2007-08 were the most serious of the previous series of similar cataclysmic events that exposed the deficiencies of global neoliberal capitalism. The global North has used Neoliberalism to contrive multiple crises that hamper Africa's sustainable development beyond previous traumas: unequal trade, trans-Atlantic slavery, and colonialism.*'

This judgement is of crucial significance in that it comes from Africans. It also sits four-square within the framework of critical events suggested earlier (Chapter 2).

My first-hand experience of seeing poverty in Africa is that it is often worst where it exists alongside conspicuous wealth. This isn't some sort of accident or coincidence. It is the predictable outcome of a ruthless Western-based economic system intended to make profits at all costs, without heed to the collateral damage it causes to families and children. European and American businesses have taken every opportunity to invest in the new Africa and make their millions there. These profits have been paid for by the cuts African countries have been forced to make in public services such as health, welfare and education. The process has been identical to how the British government, headed by David Cameron and his Chancellor George Osborne, chose to respond after the financial crisis. Local authority services, including those for families with young children, were drastically cut back, and special programmes such as Sure Start, which were proven to be highly effective, were simply abandoned. All this was done deliberately for Britain to remain within the arbitrary limits required by a neoliberal policy framework. It was thought to be the only way to run the economy, regardless of the impact on the most impoverished regions and families. Their decisions are now playing out in the breakdown of public services in several major cities such as Bradford and Liverpool and the disastrous effect, seen every week, on services to protect children at risk of abuse and neglect.

In Africa, I have recently seen extraordinary examples of abject poverty in the tiny country of Eswatini (previously known as Swaziland), where families with young children live in stone-age conditions on a small island in a river and eking out an existence by catching the most diminutive of fish, hardly large enough to be called minnows. These families live no more than a dozen miles from the Royal Palace of the absolute ruler King Mswati III of Swaziland, who was privately educated in the UK and had a fleet of expensive Rolls Royce cars at his disposal. His people suffer disproportionately from tuberculosis and HIV/Aids, and their average life expectancy, at 58 years, is the twelfth lowest in the world.

In Western Uganda, I visited a woman –Gloria – who lived within sight of Fort Portal, a regional and prosperous centre. However, her house was only accessible by a track, steep and challenging to negotiate. Nearby were smart new homes with modern facilities, and roads were being cleared to build more private houses. But, as far as she was concerned, these could have been in another world. Her house was a dilapidated, leaky mud and straw property with neither furniture nor facilities.. Her life was one of absolute poverty.

Within a mile of her house are petrol stations, a regional hospital, stylish restaurants, high-end tourist hotels, and modern offices for local

Gloria's house and family

administrators and well-known aid agencies. She was doing her best to bring up her three grandchildren, orphaned due to her children's deaths from HIV/Aids a decade earlier. Her circumstances could not have shown more clearly the enormous contrast, even in Africa, between the lifestyles of a small minority who benefit from Neoliberalism and those of the vast majority of people who still live far more impoverished lives not far away from affluent city centres.

I talked to another family with six children under 16 living on the same city's outskirts. They found it incredibly difficult to survive in their rented shop, just off a busy road, which also served as their tiny house with only a single room serving as their living room and bedroom. Unlike families who live in more rural settings, this family had no land to grow anything. The young mother, Caroline (not her real name), was visibly stressed and depressed by her predicament. The cramped environment could hardly have been less conducive to providing a decent space for her children to live and grow up. And nutrition-wise, it was apparent that neither the children nor their parents had enough food to eat, let alone good and balanced diets.

Zambia provides a gross example of the savage inequality and inhumanity of Neoliberalism. Many men there work in Western-owned copper mines where extraordinary pollution arises from the smelting process used to produce copper. They and their families suffer from associated and often lethal industrial illnesses but do not receive anything remotely like the health care their working conditions demand. The incidence of child Stunting in Zambia, hardly surprising, given the impact of these very adverse circumstances on families, stands at over 40 per cent. Chief among the owners is the Swiss-based Glencore Corporation, among the richest in Europe and delivering handsome profits for its investors. And yet, in the Swiss canton where Glencore is based, residents were asked whether they would be willing to make modest contributions from their local taxes to help improve the health care available to Zambian miners and their families. They voted, predictably, against the proposal. Such is the reality of the greed and inequality that Neoliberalism represents.

In Uganda, the dramatic impact of Neoliberalism can hardly be avoided. In Kampala, the capital, several 5-star Luxury hotels are equipped with swimming pools, in-room massage service, air conditioning, and restaurants indistinguishable from those in America or Europe. Their very names – Emin Pasha, Kampala Serena, and Hilton, tell the story of their origins and purpose. They are there to facilitate the importation of capital funds from the West and oversee the construction of expensive shopping malls equipped with 'elevators' – unknown to most Ugandans – and smart coffee houses no different from those in Milan, London, and Chicago. They are the face of the new Kampala – a city in which smart-suited business people – the 1 per cent – do their deals, negotiate franchises about the spread of American fast food outlets, and work out contracts about the export of Ugandan coffee, tea, and oil. And all at prices that make attractive profits for companies in the USA and Europe but do nothing to help the rest of the population – the ninety-nine per cent of families and their children in Uganda whose interests are not seen as being of any relevance to the neoliberal objective of making profits for the few. What is particularly obscene in Uganda is that these apparent signs of neoliberal 'success' are very often adjacent to the inner-city slums of Kampala, where families are living in rat-infested squalor without sanitation and where young children play in sewage-filled streams and where 'houses' are built of, at best, corrugated metal sheets and often just odd pieces of plywood or broken pallets or railway sleepers.

The new and ugly face of Western greed and inequality is there in full view in this and other capital cities. The predicament of families and children living in such dreadful surroundings speaks volumes about how Uganda and other countries in sub-Saharan Africa, including Kenya and South Africa, choose

Child playing by a polluted stream in Kampala

their priorities. The World Bank and the immensely wealthy and mainly American companies who profit so much from their investments in sub-Saharan Africa should, along with their political partners in the governments of these countries, be aware of and take responsibility for the damage they cause to the health and wellbeing of the majority of the families of these nations, whose children deserve far better.

These examples of the difference between rich and poor in Africa are the direct consequences of Neoliberalism. I have not found any evidence that the concept of 'trickle down' has brought any beneficial effects to improve health, inequality, or childhood nutrition. Even the most ardent proponents of this ideology surely never envisaged that squalor and misery on this scale would have been the end product of their efforts. Or perhaps they have done precisely that and see it as some necessary stage in 'modernising' Africa and making cities more like clones of their American counterparts.

Writing about Cameroon in West Africa, Horatio Clare,[2] a British travel writer, gives a graphic example of how French logging companies, such as Rougier, have illegally plundered the rainforests without regard to its environmental damage or its impact on local communities. Similar and well-documented accounts of Western destructiveness in Liberia and Nigeria at the hands of Goodyear and BP show how determined many international companies have been in their pursuit of profits in ways that would not be tolerated in America or Europe. There is little regulation about how companies can operate in Africa, which opens up loopholes for foreign businesses to exploit and make much greater profits than in the West. A few 'rotten apples' can't explain this. Even companies such as BP, Goodyear, Nestle, Glencore and Unilever, who value their reputations in Europe and America, have acted unfairly in the way they have disregarded African workers' rights and environmental standards, let alone the law, in their pursuit of profits across the region.

The scale of the West's dominance over Africa in the post-independence era can't be overestimated. It hasn't been confined even to the large multinational companies mentioned above. According to Kwame Nkrumah and Susan Williams, it has also involved the so-called 'American Military – Security complex', working behind the scenes on a large scale to ensure supplies of essential metals such as uranium, coltan, plutonium and cobalt are secured for their use in nuclear weapons or high-end smartphones and communications equipment. These issues have made African countries ever more subservient to the West and vulnerable to foreign political and financial interference in their affairs. This can be seen particularly in how France continues to be involved in Mali and the Central African Republic, the United States in DRC, and Portugal in Angola.

British researcher Jorg Wiesgratz[3] draws attention to the contrast between how neoliberals praise Uganda for having one of the world's fastest-growing economies – second only to India – while being widely criticised by respected economists and sociologists for the way, he concludes, that Neoliberalism has impacted negatively on the lives of so many of its citizens and their families. That there are such diametrically opposite narratives gives serious cause for concern about the facts about Neoliberalism's benefits, especially when, as described above, the reality for most families and children in Uganda is all too damaging and apparent.

It is heartbreaking for this writer to see first-hand how this African government has deliberately embarked on this transition from traditional African values of communitarianism to American-style market and individualism being applied to every activity.

But before leaving this section about the shortcomings of Neoliberalism and modern capitalism, it is worth looking at what is often seen as the liberal alternative – the giving of aid by the West to poor African nations. It is astonishing as well as ironic to know that it is the World Bank – the same organisation that killed off the idea of Primary Health Care when the WHO had proposed it in the late '70s- which is now in the vanguard, not just of those promoting Neoliberalism across the Global South, but of actually giving guidance to these self-same countries as to how they might reduce the incidence of poverty and child malnutrition.

In cities such as Nairobi, Kampala and Johannesburg, it is only too obvious to see the face of what might be called 'The Aid Industry,' where, in the more fashionable and expensive districts, the plush offices of the larger international aid organisations from the UN, UNICEF, Oxfam, Save the Children, and other similar organisations proliferate, and where their white Toyota Land Cruisers are parked. It is evident that in these areas, Foreign Aid is big business. This is not to completely write off these and other agencies, but it raises questions about their numbers and the ultimate justification for their roles and existence.

One argument for their being is based on the rebuilding work in wartorn Europe and Japan after WW2 when entire countries' infrastructure had been destroyed. This was done under the Marshall Plan to help the affected countries get back on their feet economically and socially. This kind of aid, based on repayable loans, was highly successful, as shown in the dramatic post-war reconstruction in Germany and Japan, where entire industries and economies had been wrecked. But these rebuilding plans differed from what is being done in the Third World through international aid in that their work was primarily short-term and highly focussed on economic and, in some cases, political regeneration, as distinct from the ongoing and broad brush and often uncoordinated activities in which most aid agencies are typically involved. Although some NGOs are conspicuously successful in their work – WaterAid being such an example – it is hard to cite any country where external aid has been of critical and strategic importance in helping to achieve significant 'structural' changes in any way comparable to the dramatic changes made in the post-war period. Most donor countries' governments are aware of these criticisms and are now working to ensure that their contributions are made more thoughtfully than in the past. The argument remains, though, as to whether international aid, at least in its current form, is such a good idea, and outspoken African economists such as Dambisa Moyo[4] are pressing for much greater emphasis to be placed on reforms that will deliver sustained political and economic improvements in poorer nations.

With passion, she writes: 'Evidence overwhelmingly confirms that aid to Africa has made the poor poorer and the growth slower. She argues that a failure to make this shift exposes developing countries to continued corruption and poverty and declining public services standards, including health and education:

> *The insidious aid culture has left African countries more debt-laden, inflation-prone, and unattractive to higher-level investment. It's increased the risk of civil conflict and unrest. Aid is an unmitigated political, economic and humanitarian disaster.'* She does not argue for isolationism and concludes: *'There has never been a greater need for constructive international engagement on the continent. Besides, the global economy could reap significant rewards from positive engagement.*

Her view of 'constructive international engagement' may not be as realisable as she envisages. Western investors have been completely determined to make their profits, whether in terms of African mineral wealth or agricultural products. Aside from missionaries, whose own motives may sometimes be questionable, they showed no regard for Africans or their children's well-being or nutrition.

The phenomenon of contemporary Chinese aid to Africa is worth attention. Unlike the colonialists of the last century and Western investors today, China is investing in Africa very differently. It is working long-term on infrastructure programmes such as trunk roads or railway systems that will be of genuine strategic significance to host countries rather than merely vehicles to maximise Chinese profits tomorrow. Perhaps in working like this, they are drawing on their own hard-won experience of modernisation both in terms of health care as well as economics and, at the same time, planting the seeds of a new relationship that forward-thinking African leaders can trust more than the one with the West which has proved so one-sided and exploitative. Chinese 'aid' isn't particularly benevolent and, perhaps, was never intended to be. Because it seems to come out of that country's history and experience and its unique and decidedly non-colonial tribulations before WW2, it might, arguably, better assist Africa as it makes a similar journey out of poverty and oppression

African countries which have been successful in moving out of poverty, including Botswana, Rwanda, Ghana, Ethiopia and South Africa, are offered as examples of the way ahead, in contrast to Angola, the Democratic Republic of Congo and Zambia, where corruption has been rife and where their leaders have embezzled eye-wateringly large amounts of foreign aid.

There are very polarised views about Neoliberalism and its impact on SSA. Some see it as offering new ways of managing national economies, as has happened in America and much of Europe. Still, a very different picture emerges when measured, not in aggregate national budgets, but about how ordinary people are affected. For example, neo-liberals might conclude that Nigeria, Uganda and Zambia are prosperous nations with healthy growth rates and above-average earnings. But, looking below the surface of these numbers, it is a fact that in each of these countries, family poverty levels are extraordinarily high, as are the proportions of children suffering from malnutrition and ill health. Statistics about the value of exports such as oil, tea and coffee, or copper – to list the main export products for each of these nations, gives a very partial picture of the reality of life for most citizens.

Notes and Further Reading
In *'he Looting Machine* (2015),[5] Tom Burgess, a *Financial Times* journalist, colourfully exposes the systematic theft of Africa's wealth by legitimate but

ruthlessly profiteering international companies, including Unilever, Coca-Cola, and Glencore, as well as by billionaire businessmen like Dan Gertler and corrupt national leaders such as Robert Mugabe, the recently deceased President of Zimbabwe.

Poverty and Neoliberalism (2007)[6] by Ray Bush, Emeritus Professor of African Studies and Development Politics at Leeds University, is a masterpiece of clarity about neoliberalism's insidious impact in the Global South. He cogently demonstrates how poverty and malnutrition in Africa sustain western wealth and power despite the World Bank's rhetoric. This is essential reading and provides a thoroughly researched analysis of how SSA continues to be entrapped in poverty by the West decades after the end of colonialism.

In *The Price of Inequality*, Joseph Stiglitz, the Nobel Prize-winning economist and a former Chief Economist at the World Bank, has warned about the damage that neoliberalism creates, both in the USA and the developing world. He makes repeated references to how the wealthiest 1per cent have dominated the debate about the economy to the detriment of the 99 per cent of ordinary citizens whose life chances are far less promising in every way than the wealthy elite. These warnings from such a respected and authoritative source cannot be ignored. They powerfully confirm much of this book's message about the harmful impact that Western policies have on poorer countries, especially when, as in the case of many countries in SSA, neoliberal policies have been imposed on them.

In *Home in the World*, Nobel laureate Amartya Sen[7] writes about the pernicious impact of British colonialism on India, where India's economy was stifled during 200 years of British rule, and famines were commonplace. Since independence in 1947, he states, there have been no famines, and democracy has prospered.

Globalisation has been the latest phase of international capitalism to affect Africa. It is described as 'The New Scramble for Africa' and represents how wealthier nations and companies are competing to extract even greater profits from Africa. In his 2016 book of the same name, Irish geographer Padraig Carmody, op cit, gives many examples of how this ruthless process has been continued, with, as always, no heed being given to how these deals might affect families and children. He concludes with these words: *Ultimately, it is Africans, in collaboration and in conflict with each other, who will determine whether resource dependence or authoritarianism on the continent can be overcome.*

The highly regarded South Korean economist Ha-Joon Chang, now at Cambridge, is sceptical about neoliberalism and challenges many of the myths frequently and inaccurately used to criticise African governments and their country's lack of economic growth. As he points out in *23 Things they don't tell you about Capitalism* (2010), many of the 'failures' of African politicians and their shortcomings were features of the past economic policies pursued by the USA and Western nations. One example is how many Western countries were protectionist and resistant to ' free trade' when their infant industries were growing. In two other books, *Bad Samaritans – the Guilty Secrets of Rich Nations* (2007, Random House) and *Kicking Away the Ladder* (2003, Anthem Press), Chang vividly describes how the wealthier nations are preventing developing countries from adopting the very same policies that they themselves used when their industries and economies were growing.

The advocates for neoliberalism and globalisation make a case for all nations to participate in worldwide trade. In *Globalisation, Poverty and Inequality*, the economist and writer Raphael Kaplinsky[8] has examined the evidence for and against the benefits of Globalisation for poorer countries. He concludes that the workings of globalisation *'condemn many people to poverty, particularly those living in Africa, Latin America and the Caribbean.'*

He has carefully looked at China's contribution to SSA during his academic career and remains highly sceptical as to whether, and despite their history and beliefs, they will offer any more than the West has done.

Section 3

The overall Impact on children of Western interventions in Africa and what must be done now

Chapter 9

A summary of how these events have together affected African children

The preceding chapters have demonstrated that Africa's position in today's world and the predicament of its children owe almost everything to the history of its one-sided relationship with the West. The extraordinarily high levels of child malnutrition and mortality presently experienced by African children have come about entirely as a result of the ways – essentially exploitative – in which the wealthier nations have treated African countries and families over recent centuries and up to the present day.

Although these episodes have been described separately in the first part of this book, it has been the cumulative effect of these crucial Western interventions that has led to the present levels of malnutrition and child deaths. These have amounted to a sustained assault by the West on an entire region of the African continent. The consequences for families and their children reflect the remorseless greed of the European powers, including Britain.

Beyond question, it was the period of slavery-described in Chapter 3 – that embedded prejudice and racism so profoundly and ever since into Western thinking and behaviour. It was born out of a combination of ignorance and avarice. There was no reason for Westerners to feel superior to Africans, and early visitors did not. On the contrary, they experienced positive and mutually rewarding relationships with Africans on trading and personal terms. They reported back positively on Africans as immensely skilled builders and creative artisans. Later, Western visitors and colonialists found this hard to believe even when faced with the evidence of African achievements. They thought Africans were 'primitive and uncivilised' people who did not warrant the most basic respect. This pivotal shift of belief led to the West embarking on scarcely credible behaviours, which, for centuries, led to the deaths and appalling mistreatment of Africans, whether as enslaved people or those families left behind. The active involvement of the European Christian churches and even of the British Royal family in the growth of the Atlantic slave trade should not be underestimated. The nightmarish impact on African children hardly needs further emphasis. Either they were left without fathers or mothers, or their families were exposed to constant fear from marauding slavers. It is hard to believe that such barbarities were ever supported and even justified by the West. It seems incredible that it took so long for Britain to abandon the practice and that many people in power resisted its abolition.

So toxic and racist were the attitudes that had developed during the slave trade that even after abolition, European leaders felt no compunction at the end of the nineteenth century in deciding unilaterally to divide the continent. They believed it unnecessary to consult or involve local leaders in this process. They had no reservations about their methods of ignoring African sovereignty, taking ownership of their lands, and treating them and their families in any way they thought fit. As outlined in Chapter 4, colonisation was the episode when Western hegemony and domination prospered in every part of the region. The record of the European powers was frequently callous and, often, murderous, with colonisers being concerned mainly with how much profit they could make from the human, agricultural and mineral resources they controlled by the force of arms. African families and their children's health and well-being didn't figure at all in their calculations. In some colonies, native populations were vastly reduced due to the inhumanity shown towards them by the Europeans, most egregiously and murderously by Germany in Southwest Africa, Belgium in Congo, Britain in Kenya and South Africa, and by Portugal in Angola, when working conditions were imposed that were highly detrimental to families and children. The last years of British colonisation of Kenya in the 1950s resulted in what became known as Britain's 'Gulag' involving the mass torture of African freedom fighters, described as *'evidence of how a society warped by racism can descend into casual inhumanity.'*

Many colonial administrators took their responsibilities very seriously, for example, as District Officers. But they were inevitably figures of foreign authority overseeing the conduct of their 'subjects' and always without their consent.

When African countries became independent, as described in Chapter 5, the West and the USA frequently disregarded their lawful rights. They used their financial and military superiority to impose their way of doing things or even, in the case of Congo/Zaire, even on their choice of leaders. Compared to these episodes, very little was done during this neo-colonial period to improve local health standards, nutrition or education for Africans and their children. They were considered insignificant compared to Western geopolitics and their settlers' health, well-being and profits. In other countries, and most notoriously in DRC/Zaire and Angola, newly independent nations were not permitted to become fully autonomous when their leaders or politics displeased the American government. Chapter 5 provides more details of this Neo-Colonial period in which, as predicted by Kwame Nkrumah, the former colonial powers failed to respect the independent status of their former colonies.

Many SSA countries are in thrall economically to Western governments due to World Bank 'assistance' and the questionable conduct of companies such as Glencore, Goodyear and BP in Zambia, Liberia and Nigeria, and Unilever in DRC.

As described in Chapter 6, the record of "Tropical Medicine' in contributing to African child health and well-being was, at best, undistinguished. Most of its practitioners' efforts were focused on the health needs of expatriates and their children. Western-trained doctors took little interest in the contribution that 'native medicine' could play in treating diseases or helping people cope with illness or grief and in being a significant part of African beliefs and culture. Western doctors frequently made things worse than before. The example of how rinderpest was treated best illustrates how colonialists failed to appreciate how native farmers knew how to minimise this disease's impact on their animals and themselves.

Some of Tropical Medicine's earlier efforts, especially in research, frequently raised significant ethical issues. An example of this was shown in the abusive procedures used in dealing with black children in nutritional research, which would not have been contemplated with their white counterparts. Few, if any, medical practitioners seemed able or ready to appreciate the significance of the environmental circumstances of African children – most notably their ignorance about poverty and sanitation/hygiene as critical factors in their lives. Even now, hospital doctors in Africa seem less aware of or concerned about chronic conditions such as stunting and malnutrition. The legacy of large hospitals left by European colonial powers has cast a long shadow over African health services, leaving huge gaps in service provision today.

The failure of the WHO's bold proposals to develop Primary Health Care (PHC) as the basis for health care services globally in the 1970s and 1980s, as described in Chapter 7, stands as the most significant and tragic setback for child health. The blame for this can be laid firmly at the door of the World Bank and its then-President Robert McNamara. They and their compliant partners at the Rockefeller Foundation and academics at several American universities lacked the vision to see the great opportunities that primary health care could have offered to millions of children across sub-Saharan Africa and South-East Asia. Instead, selective Primary Health Care (SPHC) was chosen as a cheaper option by an unholy alliance between UNICEF, and the World Bank, which led to millions of African children's lives being quite needlessly lost and which the timely adoption of PHC could have prevented.

African mothers are no less capable of caring for their babies than their Western counterparts. Nor are African children more prone to becoming ill than their Western counterparts. Without this being understood and accepted, thinking about what will be needed to bring about positive change is impossible. There cannot, otherwise, be an honest and effective dialogue between today's wealthy nations and Africa. But, of course, people in the West will say, 'Slavery and colonisation happened a long time ago, centuries even, so why can't Africa and Africans move on, as the rest of the world has done?'

Colonialism and slavery are indeed long past events. Nevertheless, these and the West's other actions described earlier have left an indelible mark on attitudes to race, still very evident today.

It took a further phase – that of Neo-Liberalism – described in Chapter 8 – to allow Europe and America to take effective control of the economies of most African countries and enable them to secure ever greater access to the mineral and agricultural resources of the sub Continent. This last step, led by the World Bank and the IMF, has placed almost every country under Western domination. The balance of trade between SSA countries and the West, including Britain, is skewed massively in favour of the West.

The profits from this remorseless process have gone overwhelmingly to the West and have left Africa in poverty. It hardly needs stating that this has, in turn, been the prime cause of family impoverishment and children's ill health and high mortality that is the subject of this book.

I have observed highly profitable Western-owned sugar companies arbitrarily refusing to pay local farmers in Kenya for their sugar cane crops because of 'cash problems', leaving farmers without any income from their crops for months until the companies arbitrarily decide when to pay for the raw sugar, long after it has been processed, packaged and sold in the West.

During the '60s and '70s, many Whites moved to Rhodesia and South Africa, given the racist policies that were attractive and actively pursued in both these countries. For them, nations were defined primarily by borders that delineated one country from another rather than by the ethnic groups who had historically lived in an area.

In the course of the current 'Black Lives Matter' campaign in the USA and the recent public re-examination of Slavery, debates have been disappointingly limited to local issues such as Black representation on company boards and in the media or about how police officers should be trained. Little is being said in Europe or America about dealing with more essential fundamentals such as reparations or admissions of responsibility for the continued poverty of sub-Saharan Africa, especially the levels of child mortality and malnutrition seen across the region. Efforts to bring about broader global change through, for example, the recent G8, 'Gleneagles' initiative led by Tony Blair, have not been markedly successful. Given its self-interested stake in maintaining inequality, the West seems unlikely to be willing to compensate Africa for the wrongs it perpetrated upon the continent, either in the form of slavery and aggressive colonialism or the imposition of neoliberal policies on African governments. The best that can be hoped for from today's Britain appears to be a gradual lessening of racist attitudes and step-by-step improvements in how African history is understood and more accurately reflected in changed curricula in schools and colleges. Countries other than the UK appear to be ahead in their willingness to do this. Belgium struggles to deal with the sickening atrocities frequently committed during King Leopold's era. Yet, even there, efforts are now being made to face up to and admit to the absolute horror of that time and not blame foreign agitators for misrepresenting what happened in Congo.

Germany has also recently acknowledged its responsibility for the genocide that it oversaw in South West Africa and is currently attempting to make some reparation for that brutal and long-lasting episode.

Because of the continuing concerns about Algeria's French policies, President Macron has recently announced that a 'Memories and Truth Commission' will be set up, primarily to review French colonial history in Algeria. This will involve 'closed' archives being opened to establish a 'recognition of the facts' and a 'reconciliation of memories'. Artefacts and documents are to be returned from Paris to Algiers.

These very recent initiatives are potentially of groundbreaking importance and could be a model for other Western countries to consider. However, such admissions have not been replicated in the UK, whose own colonial exploitation and record of brutality in Africa is still not widely known. Perhaps the historical facts of British colonialism are too embarrassing or costly, even now, for the government to contemplate.

That being said, organisations such as WHO and the United Nations, and international Non-Governmental organisations such as UNICEF, Oxfam, Cafod, and Save the Children, together with a worldwide research community, do now have impressive commitments to work with African nations to assist them in tackling the enduring problems of poverty, malnutrition, and ill-health.

Notes and Further Reading

The Newsletters freely available online from the UN initiative 'Scaling Up Nutrition' make essential reading and – most recently and encouragingly – show that real progress is being made, building on the lessons learned from countries such as those cited earlier (Chapter 10). They state, 'A world with no malnutrition is still within reach.'

Africa's Liberation, The Legacy of Julius Nyerere (2010), Edited by Chambi Chachage and Annar Cassam[1]
This collection of essays by and about Mwalimu Nyerere gives a good account of the breadth of his writing and interests. Alongside Kwame Nkrumah, he was one of the great intellectuals and internationalists to emerge from the decades of colonialism. His vision for a liberated and fully independent Africa came through powerfully and vividly in everything he wrote (see Chapter 11).

Chapter 10

How is Africa starting to deal with the legacy of child ill health, malnutrition and high mortality caused by the West's predations?

The wealthy nations of the Northern hemisphere have caused immense damage to the countries, peoples and children of sub-Saharan Africa, culminating in widespread malnutrition and enormous numbers of infant deaths. When the Allies forced similar levels of destruction upon Germany and Japan in the Second World War, massive and successful efforts were made through the Marshall Plans after 1945 to help rebuild these countries and their economies so that their futures would not be permanently blighted. Unfortunately, there are no signs that similar efforts will likely be invested in the reparations needed to achieve the permanent changes to make up for centuries of exploitation and pillage. Efforts have been made to persuade the G20 nations to cancel the debt repayments of developing countries for one or two years due to their additional problems due to Covid 19. But even these modest proposals are not certain to be accepted, which is a depressing indication of the low priority most Western nations still give to sub-Saharan Africa.

During the current global concerns about the impact of global warming, minimal action is being planned to mitigate its effects on poorer nations even when, as in the case of SSA, their poverty was brought about as a result of Western subjugation and exploitation.

In complete contrast to this somewhat depressing picture, a much more hopeful initiative is being led by the UN to deal with child malnutrition more systematically. This is 'Scaling Up Nutrition', also referred to as 'SUN'.

This programme was initiated in 2000 with the ambitious global mission of eliminating all forms of malnutrition by 2030. By 2018 60 developing countries across the world were participating in the project. Even at that stage, it was reported that 'a sharp reduction in levels of stunting' had been achieved with particular successes in Bangladesh, Cote d'Ivoire, El Salvador, Eswatini, Ghana, Kenya, Kyrgyzstan, Liberia, and Peru, all on track to meet the World Health Assembly's target on stunting reduction. Six countries were reported as making good progress in reducing both Stunting and Wasting. Forty-two countries have prepared national nutrition plans, which are vital first stages in improving nutrition. Although this is encouraging, it is discouraging that only five African countries are thought to be on target for eliminating malnutrition by 2030.

The UN admits that 'The world is still miles away from food security and adequate nutrition for every household'. The number of people undernourished in 2017 was estimated at over 820 million.

The UN's Executive Director first responsible for overseeing this ambitious initiative, Henrietta Fore, identified four chief areas as critical to success. They are:

- First, all the affected governments must commit to the vision of making better nutrition a priority and having a single budget for that purpose.
- Second, the work to achieve the global target has to be accelerated.
- Thirdly, countries need to take a systems approach to nutrition by combining agriculture and food production efforts into sustainable food systems while incorporating improved education and social protection as critical elements.
- Fourth, and finally, to fight social and gender inequalities to improve nutrition right across the life cycle and put the nutrition of girls and women at the heart of national strategies.

While being essential and overdue components of international and national strategies, these welcome plans will not be easy to translate into practice. They will need sustained financial support and integrated and sophisticated management systems that are not common anywhere, let alone in countries where such capabilities and experience are not yet developed. But the excellent news, which flies in the face of Western indifference, is that developing nations are starting to find their own ways of dealing with their problems and not wait until help comes from their former colonisers. This is emerging from a period when many African heads of state clung to power for too long. But it is becoming clear that new leaders, such as those in Ethiopia and Rwanda, are beginning to change Africa as this older generation passes.

Following are four examples of countries in sub-Saharan countries where good progress is being made to substantially and sustainably reduce child malnutrition and child deaths.

Malawi

This small, landlocked, and impoverished country, the 174th poorest of 181 countries globally, formerly known as Nyasaland, was a British Colony until 1964. Its fraught history includes slavery at the hands of the Portuguese and Arabs and a weak economy mainly based on ivory and food exports.

Malawi may seem a somewhat unlikely country to have substantially improved its children's health and well-being. Perhaps, though, it is precisely because of its size and complex history that so much progress has been made, to a point where Malawi managed to reach the UN millennium target MDG 4 (reducing under 5's mortality by 2/3 by 2015) by 2013. Between 2001 and 2013, this resulted in about 280,000 fewer child deaths – a heart-stopping and moving achievement.

Malawi effectively coordinated the work of different departments and has made changes down to the community level. This has been done partly due to its politicians' open-mindedness in wanting to change for the better and then in the willingness of several Western countries to work together with them. These successes have eluded governments in the region's more extensive and better-off countries.

Malawi still doesn't meet all the UN Sustainable Development Goals (SDG) changes required by 2030, but its achievements are already impressive and promising. It has been helped in its efforts by a rare combination of WHO, The World Bank, external grantmakers including the Bill and Melinda Gates Foundation, and five Western countries – Australia, Canada, Norway, Sweden and the UK – all ready to work together.

This remarkable story – against all the odds – has come about because Malawi was so desperately poor and unlikely ever to make the changes that would be needed without outside assistance. Credit goes to the government of Malawi, who recognised the gravity of the problems of hunger and malnutrition faced by so many children and families there and saw that they were not realistically going to be able, without outside assistance, to make the radical changes that would be needed to improve matters.

In doing this, the Malawian government was one of the first in Africa to appreciate the importance of evidence-based policies as the basis for change.

The professionals who helped bring this extraordinary transformation were academics and experts from six different countries and organisations who had identified from their research both the specific causes of malnutrition and what needed to be done across sectors for these to be successfully tackled.

Under the umbrella of 'Countdown to 2015', they pooled their resources to work with the government to help Malawi achieve remarkable change and reduce infant mortality substantially. This initiative must be an encouraging and valuable example to other African countries embarking on the same journey. [5]

Senegal

With less than 16 million citizens, this tiny West African state has also been a success story in dealing with child malnutrition over the last 15 years. It has reduced stunting levels from 33 per cent to 19 per cent, one of the lowest rates in that region. As well as achieving these results relatively quickly, it has been very clear in documenting how it has gone about this, and the mechanisms should be of interest to other nations.

As in Ethiopia and Malawi, one of the fundamental keys to success has been a high level of political understanding of nutrition's crucial importance as a critical national policy priority. Given the many issues, such as Health, Education, Agriculture, Social Protection and Finance, competing for attention in all developing countries, this wasn't as straightforward as it might seem. There are many countries where it has not happened. But even when nutrition was agreed to be an overarching issue for the nation, nothing can happen in a democracy until this can be translated into genuine commitment and practical action. This might sound like 'management speak', and it could have been were it not for the evidence from Senegal that many efforts were deliberately taken to get shared support from a wider group of citizens and interest groups such as farmers, legislators, professionals, and NGO's willing to get involved in what might be called the 'nutrition community'. Again, it is clear that there was an understanding that even this would not be sufficient to get things done in Senegal. Some other mechanism was needed to bridge ideas and proposals about nutrition with the organisational structure of government. This became a coordinating body for Nutrition – the CLM (Cellule de Lutte contre la Malnutrition) – which was accommodated in the Prime Minister's office. This proved to be an essential and powerful body, with significant influence and connections to other government sectors from Health and Agriculture to Women's Entrepreneurship and Finance. Simultaneously, a new national nutritional programme, PRN, 'Programme de Reinforcement de la Nutrition', was set up with a 15-year plan, which worked right across the country's 45 local districts and every sector. Initially, the World Bank contributed 90 per cent of costs with 10 per cent from the government, but from 2016, the running costs were shared equally. By 2015 this thoughtful and deliberate multisectoral approach led to more specific plans and timescales for work in 4 main areas; food production, food processing, education and hygiene, and health and nutrition services. This ambitious change process has enabled this tiny country to make substantial progress. Between 2000 and 2016, Senegal and several other West African countries, including Ghana, Cameroon, Togo and Angola, reduced malnourishment, child wasting and stunting, and child mortality by up to 56 per cent.

The cross-sector and systematic approach has been extraordinarily impressive in diversifying diets and improving health to a much greater extent than in the past, when most efforts were directed at reducing food staples' prices.[3]

Rwanda

Rwanda suffered the most dreadful horrors of internecine mass murders just a quarter of a century ago when the Tutsis, a minority group of its people, embarked on a killing spree that led to over half a million Hutus deaths in that country. There had been a long history of such atrocities which had fuelled this most recent episode, in full view of the world's press.

It looked impossible for Rwanda to recover from this. Still, quite remarkably, this has been possible due to the strong leadership of its President, Paul Kagame and the extensive involvement of the World Bank, the Bill and Melinda Gates Foundation and UNICEF, working together to make sizeable reductions in levels of child malnutrition. This was achieved by combining outside expertise, generous funding (totalling $116m), and political determination. This unique 4-year programme is set to save the lives of at least 19,000 children and prevent more than 37,000 children from becoming stunted.

It's hard to conceive of more difficult circumstances in which to tackle malnutrition than Rwanda.

Rwanda's lesson is that it is possible to significantly reduce child malnutrition levels anywhere, given national leaders' determined resolve, so long as this is combined with skillfully used external resources.[3]

Ethiopia

What has happened in Ethiopia could not have been more different than in Malawi, Rwanda and Senegal, but it is even more impressive [https://www.unicef.org/ethiopia/nutrition].[4]

Unlike Senegal, Rwanda and Malawi, Ethiopia is one of the largest African countries, with a population of over 100 million across distinct geographical regions. Its recent history has been about brutal dictatorship and civil war involving murderous divisions between what was to become Eritrea and modern Ethiopia. Not until 1992 did the country emerge from this turmoil as one of the world's poorest countries, with two-thirds of its children being stunted. In the face of what must have seemed like insuperable challenges, the new single-party government changed its mission radically. It has been unswerving in its determination to improve the lot of its people. It was recognised from the start that for this to work, all efforts had to be made on a multi-sectoral basis, right across the traditional administrative boundaries of education, transport, agriculture, finance and health. Not only were these functions made to work together at national and community levels, but external aid and NGO work were also looked at critically to ensure that these were absolutely consistent with national priorities. This step was critically important in Ethiopia. It enabled all available resources to focus more effectively on the new government's sophisticated evidence-based policies and targets. No other nation has been so determinedly single-minded, and none has been so successful in bringing about radical improvements in ordinary people's lives.

One example of this determination deserves particular attention. Offers by the World Bank to help reconstruct this battered country were rejected because Ethiopian politicians were not prepared to accept the financial restructuring that was a precondition of the offer. This was a brave decision, but it has allowed Ethiopia to pursue its own agenda and not become, as many other countries in SSA have done, subservient to the controversial neoliberalist ideology that inevitably went with the work of the World Bank.

The NGO sector's contributions have also been skilfully channelled into activities that suit the country rather than, as is very common, meeting the myriad and not necessarily comparable objectives and priorities of external funders. Again, this policy seems to make a great deal of sense and completely contrasts with the somewhat chaotic way some other countries deal with outside agencies. In Uganda, for example, there are several hundred foreign

NGOs and no apparent reason why so many have been permitted to operate there. Some support orphanage care, while others endeavour to do just the opposite – to help families stay together. That makes no sense and needs to be reviewed.

Ethiopia's committed approach is inspiring and shows what countries can achieve if there is a single-mindedness to tackle poverty, malnutrition, and child deaths together. Over the last 30 years, enormous improvements have been made. Extreme poverty has fallen from 71 per cent to 31 per cent, and farmers' yields and family incomes have doubled. Levels of malnutrition have dropped significantly, and there is now food to sell. Farmers who typically lived in mud and straw huts can now afford to live in houses made of tin and bricks.

Spending on Education has dramatically increased, and primary school enrollment has quadrupled. Boys in primary schools no longer outnumber girls. Every village offers preventive health care services, and more than 40,000 community volunteers have been trained as health extension workers. In addition, there has been a dramatic increase in the numbers of doctors and nurses being trained, so much so as to counterbalance the numbers of trained health professionals who decide to emigrate in search of higher salaries elsewhere.

Tremendous efforts have been invested in discouraging open defecation, a significant cause of disease. The proportion of people doing this has fallen from 79 per cent to 22 per cent, and those with access to improved water sources have doubled.

Although the gains in Ethiopia are impressive and have revolutionised public services in this vast country, much more needs to be done to ensure the quality of services and achieve the SDG 2030 targets for poverty, food and education. However, there is every indication that the government intends to do this and do it by adhering to the principles that have been at the heart of the changes made over almost 30 years. Ethiopia wants to attract donor support but is rightly determined to keep ownership of its agenda. Not insignificantly, China is the largest foreign investor, and even the World Bank is now a contributor, despite its initial reservations about Ethiopia's development programmes.

Two other African nations have made substantial and impressive strides in addressing child malnutrition. In Zambia, legislative changes have made it more possible for women to combine their work and family responsibilities. Workers considered as vulnerable can now claim up to 120 days of maternity leave. This has helped the country achieve one of the world's highest exclusive rates for breastfeeding at 72% between a baby's birth and reaching five months old. Kenya joined the SUN Movement in 2012, determined to take committed action to improve nutrition. This involved the launch of their first National Nutrition Action Plan and the adoption of 11 High Impact Nutrition interventions targeting the first 1000 days of a child's life. Kenya is the only country now on target to achieve the World Health Assembly targets for nutrition. This is highly impressive and demonstrates what a multi-sectoral approach can achieve. As Gerda Verburg, now leading the United Nations initiative, concludes – senior political figures have the power to convene critical sectors and ensure a 'whole government' approach to tackling the ' drivers' of malnutrition. Her former role as a senior government Minister in the Netherlands taught her that political commitment doesn't come about accidentally. It can be created and strengthened over time by strategic action. The United Nations prioritises the importance of the Scaling Up Nutrition Movement as a critical platform in bringing about sustainable improvements in nutrition in developing countries while enabling more comprehensive and structural changes in their economies. She sees the nutrition plan as the only way to drive down Stunting and unlock the potential of people, societies and nations in a way that catalyses the eventual attainment of the UN's Sustainable Development Goals by 2030. Gerda Verburg states that every dollar invested in reducing chronic malnutrition in children yields a 16-dollar return.

The lessons from these examples suggest that measurable and significant changes can be achieved only when leadership is provided at the highest levels – the Presidency – and when changes involve the entire range of government activities. They were neither envisaged nor delivered by being confined to child welfare. The danger of not observing these lessons is that changes may be cosmetic and trivial rather than fundamental, addressing symptoms rather than causes. This is not surprising because it chimes with what the WHO's Director-General, Dr Mahler, stressed four decades previously. It also echoes the experience of the changes introduced in China during the barefoot doctor era when the local delivery of health care went alongside the day-to-day practice of better treatments. A very similar conclusion was reached by a study by M.J. Azevedo (2017) [5]

His report boldly states that the prescription for improving health systems in Africa will require the World Bank, USAID and donors such as the Bill and Melinda Gates Foundation to include in their work a more balanced, horizontal approach to disease, prevention and education. Such a recommendation hasn't come too soon, given each organisation's unfortunate and long-term antagonism towards prevention and community-based health care.

Notes and Further Reading

In *Turning the World Upside Down; The search for Global Health in the 21st century* (2010), Nigel Crisp, a former Chief Executive of the NHS, has some valuable suggestions about two-way exchanges between Africa and the West.[7] These ideas are worth consideration. However, it might be wiser for the West to be more prepared to work with African leaders rather than impose their own economic and commercial dogmas upon them.

They need to recognise that the Africans are the experts and much more likely to know what changes are required for their citizens, parents and families.

This very point is splendidly elaborated in *African Health Leaders – Making change and claiming the future*, where Francis Omaswa, formerly Director-General for Health Services in Uganda and Nigel Crisp edit a collection of fascinating and perceptive essays which Dr Nksazana Dlamini-Zuma, Chair of the African Union Commission, describes as *'Essential reading for African Health leaders, about how, country by country, Africans can build on their own traditions and experience to offer health care to their own people. It is also a guide for foreign partners who want to know how best to support Africans in a spirit of global solidarity.'*[6]

Chapter 11

What more must be done to help African children?

The citizens of sub-Saharan Africa can't hold out any hope that the West is likely to come to its aid in a comprehensive way, similar to the post-WW2 Marshall Plans that would be needed to resolve the prodigious problems they face.

Even high profile and potentially game-changing Commissions, such as those led by earnest and able leaders such as Canada's Prime Minister, Lester Pearson, Germany's Chancellor, Willie Brandt and more recently by the UK's Prime Ministers, Tony Blair and Gordan Brown, have not been able to make any comprehensive and permanent difference.

Change for the better only occurs when organisations work together, as I will show later. It doesn't happen when individuals or organisations, such as spectacularly happened here, go their own way. Many well-intentioned professionals – such as teachers, doctors, researchers, engineers, and many respected international aid organizations, may unwittingly have placed their particular interests and ideologies before children's wellbeing in the developing world. In particular, the Bill and Melinda Gates Foundation has frequently gone it alone in investing too much in treating diseases rather than preventing them.

But with rare exceptions, possibly that of medical missionaries, the result of Western engagement in Africa has been to cause very significant damage and harm to the continent's children's health and well-being. Over the centuries, and as illustrated earlier, the West's hegemonic view of Africa has prevailed, and Western interests have invariably taken first place. Consequently, the conditions required to ensure African children's health and development were significantly jeopardized. Frequently, this led to sharp increases in child mortality, most notably in the eras of slavery and aggressive colonization when entire families were left to starve as their menfolk were forced to work away from their villages on distant rubber plantations for months. This led to very significant reductions in national populations. At other times, the harm has been less pronounced but still significant.

Few enduring and genuinely positive changes have occurred because the West is too compromised to act differently due to its history and its continued self-interest in profiteering from Africa. The passionate revival of concerns from the Black Lives Matter campaigns worldwide should improve how Black people are viewed and treated. President Biden's recent election in the USA might lead to American policy changes to ensure that overt discrimination against BAME citizens is reduced or made illegal. There ought to lead to less violence perpetrated by police forces, better educational opportunities for children from BAME families, and improved representation of BAME citizens in the professions and public bodies. All of this will be for the good and should start building a world where endemic and hostile prejudice is reduced between people of different backgrounds and racial heritage.

However, it seems doubtful that the West will radically change how it deals with SSA in challenging issues such as trade or investment. The attitudes that led to SSA's exploitation over the centuries are deeply and structurally embedded in the West and will not be easily altered by campaigns or lobbying. The West has direct and deeply vested interests in maintaining the wealth gap it created, which is profitable for companies, governments, and, to be blunt, most citizens.

Western citizens' comfortable living standards are substantially built on the backs of African farmers and families. Tinkering with this through decent initiatives such as Fair Trade or other labelling programmes cannot work other than at the margins. Will Western shoppers really be prepared to pay the prices for tea and coffee needed to give African children decent health and education services? Are people ready to deny themselves officially certified teak or mahogany worktops in their sleek new kitchens when they must know that these are frequently sourced from the illegal logging and destruction of African primary rain forests and that such deception is often being done with the full knowledge of Western governments and companies? For example, the logging in 2019 of 5,000 cubic metres of officially stamped but banned hardwood from Gabon by the French tropical timber company, Rougier, was carried out without permits in a well-publicised corruption scandal ending with the resignation of the vice president and other officials. But such cases are common across Africa, and the legal costs of fines are seen as the price many

Western companies are cynically willing to pay to keep their highly profitable businesses.

Although genuine reparations are not likely to be considered, It is perhaps possible that more substantial efforts will be made to treat Africa and Africans with greater respect and dignity. Some European countries, such as Germany, the Netherlands, and the Scandinavian countries, are already showing the way. Even Belgium has begun a serious debate about its colonial past and recognises that much of its wealth came from its exploitation of Congo up to that country's independence.

Although more voices within the UK now challenge racism and prejudice, it is unlikely to change fundamentally soon, and where even legitimate asylum seekers and immigrants have been treated harshly and often without regard to their rights as British citizens.

Boris Johnson, when British Prime Minister and some cabinet ministers were not even prepared to accept that Britain played a significant part in impoverishing Africa and creating the conditions leading to high levels of child malnutrition and avoidable deaths. Instead, they promoted the comforting but wholly inaccurate story that Britain played a constructive and benign role in bringing civilisation and prosperity to a primitive and uncivilised continent, despite solid evidence that this was not true. This sharp difference of opinion about Britain's colonial past has shown itself to be a very live issue. As mentioned earlier, the street protests about statues of former slave traders have been hotly debated in many cities from Bristol to Oxford and Aberdeen to Edinburgh. It is also a contentious issue in other Western countries with historical involvement with slavery or African colonies.

There have been fierce debates about the conduct of previous generations and by individuals such as Burton, Stanley, Edwin Lascelles, Edward Colston, Lord Lever, Cecil Rhodes, and King Leopold. Most present-day scholars of African history feel that the evidence strongly supports the view that earlier generations of politicians, settlers and merchants were racist and exploitative. Their actions and those of their governments now seem despicable to many people.

However, some other right-wing writers have taken a different approach. For example, and as mentioned, John Darwin praises British support for slavery and presents abolition as a credit for British 'decency'. It was anything but that. Of course, Britain has played a significant part in shaping the modern world due to being the first to embrace industrialisation or extend its influence globally, whether through trade or its ideas about democracy or religion. But it is surely wrong to deliberately omit to describe the extent of the damage these ambitions caused to all of the other nations involved.

Several other recent accounts have described the continent's recent past far less ideologically and partially than have Niall Ferguson or John Darwin. Most notable among these is *The Interest – How the British Establishment resisted the Abolition of Slavery*, a very recent and meticulously researched study by Cambridge historian Michael Taylor who writes about the extent of opposition within the British establishment to the intended 1807 legislation, which banned the slave trade. That episode in British history is often presented as evidence of the country's supposed liberal and progressive stance toward the iniquity of slavery. However, as Taylor shows, there was widespread opposition to the proposed law, not just from Caribbean plantation owners but also from Cabinet ministers, including Canning, Peel and Gladstone, and from the Duke of Wellington and King William IV. It wasn't until 1833, just four years before the realm of Queen Victoria, who strongly opposed slavery, that slavery was made illegal. When it was, the British government paid over £20 million in compensation to the slave owners, the largest ever payout by the government. At today's prices, this equates to £340 billion. No other payments have ever been paid to those enslaved or their countries of origin.

British reluctance to face the facts of colonial history can still be seen at both Oxford and Cambridge. At Oriel College in Oxford, where Cecil Rhodes had briefly been a student, there is a statue to his life and as a mark of appreciation as a college benefactor. Many present-day students want his statue removed, but the college has meekly and discreditably decided not to do this because of 'planning delays and a potential government veto'. Similar reluctance in the case of another wealthy slaver/benefactor has been shown, as described earlier, at Cambridge.

The United Kingdom, until recently, did have a better track record than the USA and many European countries by investing in developing countries at the United Nations recommended level of 0.7 per cent national budget and focusing primarily on poverty reduction. However, this has already changed due to the government's regrettable decision to merge the Department for International Development with the Foreign Office. This step owes more to the UK's vote to leave the EU than anything to do with the needs of families and children in sub-Saharan Africa. As this merger goes ahead, the development budget, protected in the past, is being raided in connection with the war in Ukraine and assisting British business interests abroad. British business prosperity and the alleviation of poverty and child malnutrition in sub-Saharan Africa are certainly not policies that sit easily together.

What should be done now?

Much of what has been said here must look very unpromising. The West has exploited Africa for centuries and right up to the present. Much of what has been done to Africa can unequivocally be described, to quote Cicely Saunders, as *Tantamount to Murder*. The responsibility for the deaths of many millions of young African people can be firmly placed at the doors of Western countries, especially Britain. But if the hard-won lessons of the last ten years in public health care are examined more closely, they can offer a template for a much brighter future for Africa and its children.

The most impressive gains in child health and well-being have been achieved where new African leaders, like those in Ethiopia, Senegal, Malawi, Rwanda, together with Zambia and Kenya, have taken firm and unequivocal control over what they have decided what needs to happen in their nations to bring about the wide-ranging but connected changes which are necessary to deal with the underlying causes of ill health and malnutrition. Only national leaders are fully entitled and in a position to do this. Whether it comes from International Aid, financial help in loans and grants, or technical expertise, all potential support providers must be prepared to play roles that substantially recognise the importance of African government leadership.

The change that cries out is that donors now need to recognise that their activities must, without exception, contribute to African governments' overall strategies. This is not to overlook the corruption that has taken place in many African countries, and outside agencies are right to want to ensure that their contributions will not end up in the private accounts of African leaders or their families. But it is time for foreign donors now to realise that the time is past when they predetermine what they want to do in SSA.

The strategies that will make a significant difference to the well-being of children in Africa must all involve robust, purposeful and data-driven partnerships between the leaders of individual African countries and donor nations or highly influential organisations such as the Gates Foundation and the World Bank, and key international bodies such as the United Nations, the World Health Organisation, and UNICEF. Enough is known from recent research about the ingredients for success in dealing with malnutrition in every country, for this is no longer an issue. A study conducted recently at Harvard can now tell us, country by country and region by region, precisely what key 'drivers' need attention to achieve significant child mortality and morbidity reductions.[1]

Genuine leadership must come from the top, i.e. the President or a Prime Minister responsible for the entire budget. Child malnutrition cannot be confined to the children it damages, as if it is just a 'child welfare' or 'health' issue. As Dr Mahler argued so presciently over forty years ago, health is inextricably and significantly linked to every country's social and economic well-being. It has to be seen in this way. A recognition of this, to put it clearly, is the vital key to economic progress, as well as ending the disgracefully high infant death rates that characterise most countries in SSA and shame the West

When Heads of State give this overall and clear lead, it is essential then for strategies to be put in place to build on the critical policy topics – these being issues such as 'food and care', 'primary education, and 'health care to construct a single integrated budget, and then to rigorously manage this to ensure that all funds and activities are directed and coordinated to focus efforts on measurably improving performance in each of these areas to contribute to a better overall and measurable health outcomes for the country, and especially for its children.'

This abbreviated summary of what must be done is not easy to describe, let alone deliver, and not enough nations are making it happen yet. Too often, there are very apparent shortcomings in managing the process. These include a failure to recognise the overall importance of child malnutrition as a problem for entire nations. It might involve a laxity in ensuring that all resources are harnessed and used effectively to alleviate malnutrition. A familiar problem lies in the rivalry and status between ministers, not confined to Africa, preventing cross-departmental action. The remedy for this has to lie with heads of state who must be ruthless in insisting on joint work across traditional organisational boundaries.

This is difficult to achieve, especially in developing countries where communications and infrastructure are under-resourced and managerial capacity is limited. But help is at hand in the shape of collaboration between the United Nations SUN initiative and Pan African networks. Both offer guidance and practical advice about how nations can reduce malnutrition levels for their children. The Gates Foundation, too, has taken a welcome and overdue new initiative, *Exemplars in Global Health* highlighting successful programmes as templates for others to learn from, if not emulate.

It has been too easy to welcome foreign money even when, in reality, it often comes with strings that can interfere and conflict with the fundamental interests of nations. The neoliberal policies so robustly pursued by the World Bank are the most obvious example and serve as a warning about the dangerously mixed messages from that organisation. Even when there are no such evident and damaging strings, foreign aid can distract what developing countries decide they most need. Only they can know what will best help their citizens. Foreign aid must contribute to achieving that goal and only be used for that purpose, as it has been so impressively in Ethiopia.

President Julius Nyerere of Tanzania, even in 1968, was thinking about how Africa might need a new revolution, profound and far-reaching, hoped that it would be nourished by the vigour and resilience of native genius and the inheritance of self-respect and innovating confidence that has carried it through past centuries of change and challenge. In saying this, he echoes the views expressed by many other writers, including Basil Davidson, John Iliffe and Ruth Finnegan,[2] who were all familiar with Africa.

At the recent (2021)meeting of the G7 nations, there was agreement about a programme to counter China's influence on more than 100 developing countries, including many in sub-Saharan Africa. This initiative was intended *'to reflect our values, standards, and way of doing things'*. While it is clear that China places a lower priority on human rights than the West, this proposal still begs the question of what the G7 leaders really mean by phrases like 'our standards' and 'our way of doing things'.

This new global initiative is both hypocritical and dishonest – based on the evidence of the West's behaviour toward African nations during the post-colonial period.

China has experienced the complex processes needed to change from poverty to modernisation and knows, too, far better than the West, how to become a modern and powerful continental-wide state from its roots as a fragmented collection of kingdoms. China may, arguably, be more able to fully appreciate the kind of aid that genuinely makes a difference to developing nations rather than the self-interested and patronising aid that has characterised much recent Western assistance. Its involvement in sub-Saharan Africa could offer a better partnership to Africa based on mutual benefits than anything that is presently likely to come from the West. This view is, admittedly, a controversial position to take. However, China's recent human rights and democracy record raises profound questions about whether it can be trusted as a reliable partner in Africa.

However, European and American politicians need to seriously reflect that, for once, African leaders, although they may not yet realise it, are now in the driving seat in deciding which bloc holds out the most promise for them. This issue may take on a renewed political urgency due to the current shortage of vital computer' chips' in the modern world. Most of these are manufactured in Taiwan, whose sovereignty is the subject of dispute between China and the USA. Also becoming a hot issue is sourcing precious materials, the so-called Rare Earths, which are the critical elements needed for their manufacture. These are found in sub-Saharan Africa and will become significant in commercial relations with the West, just as Uranium has been in the past. Western leaders must tread carefully in dealing with this and not assume, as before, that they can decide how these elements can be extracted.

There are, too, severe doubts about how some NGOs work in sub-Saharan Africa. Many have too much freedom, which can be dangerously harmful, as in the case of Watoto in Uganda. Some still participate in clandestine overseas adoptions. However, the sector can play a more vital role and bring expertise in making things happen in communities, particularly where malnutrition and ill health are of primary concern.

As illustrated earlier (Chapter 10), it takes governments to bring about strategic and nationwide change, including substantial environmental, agricultural, and health improvements. However, this doesn't mean they can do everything needed to support all communities and individual families where malnutrition is likely to be a crucial issue. NGOs can best work closely with needy and hard-to-reach communities and families. This will often need much more focussed and localised help being offered to the most vulnerable families and parents, especially if there are NGOs who can play a specialist and relevant role.

One very impressive example of this is Uganda in the work of the small but highly effective organisation 'Childs i Foundation', which is pioneering new ways to support families with stress. In the past, this often involved taking children away from their natural families and placing them in residential care or with overseas adopters. Now parents are given practical support to keep their children at home. It also finds African foster and adoptive parents for children when their biological parents cannot resume care for their children for practical reasons. This ground-breaking work has the potential to reshape the present and confusing pattern of services for children. It is already being viewed as a model which could be extended across Uganda and beyond.

Another splendid example of an NGO working specifically to help reduce malnutrition, with which I have been associated, is Home-Start Uganda's (HSU) work. This small not-for-profit organisation works with families who face various challenges – from being extremely poor to being socially isolated. It recruits and trains local volunteers, themselves parents, to work with parents and has helped them and benefitted their children's health and well-being. As an example, I saw recently in Kampala how HSU has helped single parents who were desperately poor to grow tomatoes and other crops and sell them profitably at a local market. Volunteers also supported those families without access to toilets by building pit latrines.

The simple idea behind the work of Home-Start – parents helping other parents, is not new, but it has been proven in other countries to work effectively with families facing a wide range of challenges. An even more promising and relevant partnership based on these precedents is being developed in the Kabarole region of Western Uganda, adjacent to DRC, between Home-Start Uganda and the regional hospital. Here, the hospital-based nutritionist team works collaboratively with HSU volunteers to build their knowledge about child nutrition and then share this with parents in a way that has never been attempted anywhere before. This project can potentially prevent conditions such as stunting and wasting and reduce the rates of deaths in young children, which are currently far higher than in other regions. There is already evidence that this is helping to benefit children by improving parents' awareness of the importance of their children getting better diets, increasing the number of children being breastfed, and raising children's dietary diversity levels even in these very impoverished communities.

The early results from this project, Garuga Mu'kulia, roughly translated as 'Food changes everything', are extremely promising. After eight months and with the numbers of supported families and children steadily increasing, stunting and wasting rates are reducing significantly. Even more important is that, to date, none of the 100-plus infant children has died. That is a heart-stopping finding. What is also remarkable is the level of commitment and care shown by the 50-plus local volunteers whose conscientious support of the families is at the heart of the project. This ground-breaking project demonstrates how far these volunteers, themselves parents, are willing and able to help their fellow citizens even when their contributions must be sustained over many weeks and months. Also noteworthy is that it involves particular tasks akin to those of the health care workers whose work was highlighted and praised in the much earlier projects evaluated by the WHO (see chapter 7). The critical difference in their roles is that in the current project, the focus is entirely on the health and well-being of young children. These initial findings must be made the subject of more detailed investigation and evaluation as they seem to offer significant and new insights into how stunting can be prevented and how the rates of child deaths arising from malnutrition can be reduced. It looks like the low-tech idea behind Home-Start – parents helping parents – might be 'Just Made for Africa' and has great promise across the continent, especially in the multitude of communities concerned about their children's health and well-being (see http://homestartworldwide.org).

What NGOs mustn't be used for, although they very often are, is to fill gaps or even to provide public services that ought to be the province of elected governments. A striking example of this grossly inappropriate use of NGOs in developing countries can be seen in the work of orphanages. Although this may be changing, far too many orphanages are being run by foreign NGOs who bring their own priorities and philosophies, often highly inappropriately, to run orphanages without adequate safeguards or without any thought about their proper role in the countries concerned. The care of vulnerable children ought to be one of the fundamental responsibilities of all governments, but the present mishmash and confusion of policies and of provisions, which is far too familiar in SSA, leave children exposed to inadequate and inappropriate care, including overseas adoption as well as, in too many cases, of actual abuse at the hands of an unregulated sector which can allow corrupt lawyers to find loopholes in the regulations governing overseas adoptions. This is a great pity and a missed opportunity, especially when NGOs such as those highlighted above demonstrate impressive alternatives to orphanages that chime much more powerfully with the principles of good childcare that all governments should want to endorse.

A significant and sad example of missed opportunities lies in the way in which some governments are only notionally signing up for vital global initiatives, such as the Scaling up Nutrition (SUN) programme, which has the backing of both the UN and WHO, but without ensuring that action is taken to ensure the local implementation of such well-intended enterprises. This lack of ability and resources to manage and provide change was a central theme in the Blair report about Africa. All governments find it difficult to make things happen at a local level when new policies need to be thoroughly implemented, but it takes much systematic work at all public administration levels to ensure the actual delivery of new forms of service right through to communities and families. Even Ethiopia found it challenging to deliver front-line services to a satisfactory standard after making fundamental policy changes. NGOs could play a vital role in local communities by helping to strengthen the contribution of different agencies, which can often be the key to real change, especially in the case of malnutrition.

This is an unusual example of how the challenge of joining up the work of different agencies when some of the stages in the complex process of ameliorating malnutrition can be made more achievable by using NGOs as working partners.

The first part of this book describes how the West has systematically and continuously exploited Africa since the first slaves were taken by force from their communities and transported to the Americas.

Not deterred by the enormous damage slavery caused to Africa and its children, the West continued its campaigns to pillage Africa by colonising countries against their will. It involved extracting gold, diamonds, uranium and cobalt, destroying tropical rain forests for valuable hardwoods. It also involved the exportation of coffee, tea, and sugar products, involving arduous and poorly paid work conditions and at grossly unfair prices to African farmers and their families.

In the last few decades, the World Bank and the International Monetary Fund, strongly motivated by neoliberal ideology, have pressured many African countries to accept financial help on terms that do nothing to benefit most of their citizens, but open up American companies' opportunities to make more profits. However, there seems to be a possibility that President Biden is looking to move away from neoliberalism as the basis for America's economy. That would be excellent news for the poorer countries of the world.

Many opportunities to improve health services in many parts of the continent or prevent disease and children's illnesses have been missed or ignored over the years in favour of hospital-based medicine and commercially profitable treatment approaches.

Together, these actions have led to unacceptable levels of malnutrition and poor health across the region and have caused enormous harm to its children.

Although the damaging impact of Western interventions on children in SSA, as outlined here, is beyond dispute, there is little evidence that Western governments are looking to take their responsibility seriously enough to offer adequate reparation for their colonial pasts. Most prefer to deny their exploitative colonial histories, including Italy, Portugal, and the UK. A few, including Germany and even Belgium, are starting to acknowledge their past exploitation of SSA.

The British government must recognise the established facts about Britain's historic and wholesale complicity in slavery. It also needs to accept that it has played a large part in Sub-Saharan Africa's continuing impoverishment and contributed to the exceptionally high numbers of avoidable child deaths in Africa. Most concerning is that this issue is being dealt with unwisely by the government, which seems determined to repress proper and factual debate. Highly respected organisations, including national charities, museums and universities, feel that they are being threatened if they speak the truth.

It is astonishing to see just how much effort is being invested by the government to 'whitewash' Britain's past involvement in slavery. The recent report, 'Race and Ethnic Diversities', mentioned earlier, has sought to minimise the significance of slavery as it still resonates so significantly today in many parts of British life. It even claims that slavery paved the way for its survivors to become more resilient and develop and strengthen their African/British identity. As many historians have pointed out, these were the arguments advanced by slave owners to defend themselves against accusations of inhumanity.

'Race and Ethnic Diversities' tries to question the experience of racism by many people of colour in Britain and attempts to write a new 'narrative'. It even goes so far as to suggest that Britain is a model for a racially diverse nation. It also flies in the face of many earlier reports on race issues in the UK, all of which have acknowledged racism's painful reality. The broader significance of this blatant attempt to change British history is that it feeds and attempts to justify further cuts in Britain's foreign aid budget.

As described above, Slavery's impact was not confined to enslaved people. It also left much of Southern Africa socially and economically devastated and created a legacy of long-term impoverishment, still visible in extraordinary levels of child deaths and malnutrition. The government has recently decided to play down its work with 'developing' countries by setting aside its legal responsibility to spend 0.7 per cent of its GDP on overseas aid. This has been done, it is said, because of the financial crisis brought about by the Covid Pandemic and may be a temporary measure. However, by refusing to acknowledge the facts about Britain's involvement in slavery, colonialism and neoliberalism and their continuing impact on Africa, the government is undermining and withdrawing its former commitments to aid. This decision will have a devastating effect on the countries that have been so impoverished and will lead to many more children dying across sub-Saharan Africa before their fifth birthdays.

Last words

The first part of this book has outlined – perhaps too frankly for many – how the West, stage by stage, has impoverished SSA and caused lethal harm to many millions of its children. There needs to be an acknowledgement of the truth of this history if we are to move forward radically differently. Such a step would allow the West, and in particular Britain and the USA, to move away from greedy and often corrupt exploitation and towards genuine collaboration and partnership to assist more systematically with Africa's economic and social development.

The time has now come for African leaders to take total responsibility for their nations' futures and pursue this task more determinedly. As a top priority, they must ensure that their children no longer face such poor prospects as they have for far too long.

The evidence that this is now possible is clear. As amply demonstrated in Malawi, Senegal, Rwanda and Ethiopia, and now in Zambia and Kenya, leaders have the power to change that. When they take action across the range of responsibilities of governments, it is not only children who benefit and grow into healthy students and capable parents and workers. As Dr Mahler predicted, their communities and economies will also become more robust and capable of dealing with the challenges already threatening Africa, such as Covid and the Ukraine war's impact on food prices. Looming behind these are the immense implications of global warming, which will lead to continent-wide food shortages unless urgent remedial action is taken quickly.

Together with Pan-African developments, in which Africans are starting to take complete control over the continent's extensive and valuable resources, this can herald a promising and dynamic future for its people and put an end to the poverty and inequality that have been for so long regarded as acceptable and even normal.

The most encouraging example of this can be seen in the recent decision by over forty African nations assisted by the United Nations in agreeing to form an African Continental Free Trade Area. This groundbreaking initiative will reduce intercountry tariffs on many goods and products moving between countries across the continent. It will open up a huge market of over 1.2 billion people with a combined GDP of more than £3 trillion. It will enable African countries to trade equitably and use the continent's resources for Africans instead of relying on historic and one-sided trade with the West. Over time, this will reduce families' prices to pay in their local shops and greatly benefit parents in feeding their children and preventing malnutrition.

The most urgent next step for all African leaders is to take the lead, country by country, through the United Nations SUN programme to give their children a far better start in life. They have it within their power to start this transformation. Because of their history as exploiters, the Western countries now owe it to SSA's government leaders to help them make the necessary changes. This process has already been shown to be effective in several countries. Ensuring that children, girls as much as boys, are healthy and better educated will be the best way to guarantee the continent's future prosperity and overcome the past exploitation caused by the West for so long. Nothing is more important than this; no country on earth can prosper when its children are so dreadfully disadvantaged in their early years. Estimates of the financial cost of child malnutrition for the GDPs of affected countries range from 3-10%

Other than in Kenya, where British culpability was exposed for all to see, the United Kingdom has done nothing to offer proactive reparations to any of its former colonies. However, when speaking at a recent ceremony to mark the end of Barbados's links to the UK and its transition to become a separate republic, HM King Charles, when still the Prince of Wales, described the era of slavery as a 'stain' on British history. He also stated that if any of the members of the Commonwealth decide to become republics, they should be allowed to do so 'without rancour'. In doing this, he went ahead of the present government. There might be a moment when the new Monarch and Prince Willam, his son, the present and future heads of the British Royal family, could make their regrets about and apologies for their family's historical involvement in slavery in Africa more explicit. Doing this would certainly need the willing consent and support of the government, although this is most unlikely at present. What it would do, though, is to send a clear signal that Britain wants to turn a corner on its Imperial past and take a different direction in its relationship with sub-Saharan Africa, which could even lead to a new and mutually beneficial Trade Agreement between the UK and Africa. It would also greatly assist in the broader implementation of the changes still needed to tackle child malnutrition, lessen some of the associated financial problems that this causes to African nations, and enable Britain to reshape more broadly the nature and scale of its links with Africa. Even without such significant bilateral developments, Britain should still be able to offer technical assistance to those African countries that haven't yet signed up to participate in the SUN movement. This would be one of the most sensible priorities for any British government to take in deciding how best to use the 0.7 % of its GDP, which has until recently been historically and legally set aside to aid poorer countries.

By 2030 every country should achieve the internationally agreed Strategic Development Goals (SDGs)and related health targets. This will involve the SSA countries working collaboratively with Western funders and the United Nations. In turn, the Western countries, especially Britain and the USA, should acknowledge their part in the harm caused to African children, and be ready to commit more fully to working with all African nations through SUN to ensure that today's children are well nourished and healthy. It can, as shown here, be done and would save millions of young lives across the region. It will be important in this journey to fine-tune this process so that it can be sensitive enough to recognise and adapt to local differences of need and provision within each country. Even in the smallest nations, there are areas where malnutrition and child deaths are exceptionally high. Action plans must identify these and ensure that macro strategies do not overlook these local hot spots, such as those in Western Uganda that have been described. Large hospitals should no longer be allowed to dominate health provision as they have in the past. Far better, in Africa, as was argued decades ago, is for smaller hospitals to serve as community hubs, serving local needs and putting a much greater emphasis on prevention by using local resources and active citizen involvement.

The first part of this book describes in detail the part played by the West over many centuries in impoverishing sub-Saharan Africa and severely harming its children. It can only hinder future collaboration and progress if these facts are denied. The later chapters show how changes are already being made to give far more priority to adequately nourishing children across the region, especially in their early years. That overriding and crucially important objective is still far from being realised, but it can and must be so that the curse of infant deaths can be made history and allow the enormous potential of Africa and its children to be realised. The significance and benefits for African children and nations that will accrue from this can hardly be overstated. It represents a monumentally important and long overdue goal which must be achieved. If this book helps in any way to accomplish this, it will have fully served its purpose.

References

Preface
1 Black, R et al. *Global, Regional, and national trends in under -5 mortality between 1990 and 2019 with scenario-based projections until 2030:a systematic analysis by the UN Interagency Group for Child Mortality Estimation*. London: The Lancet, 2022

Introduction
1 David Livingstone, *The Life and African Explorations of David Livingstone (1874)*, London: Cooper Square Press, 2002

Chapter 1
1 World Health Organization, United Nations Children's Fund (UNICEF), World Bank, *Levels and trends in child malnutrition*, New York, 2021
2 Hughes, G et al. *The costs of adaptation to climate change for water infrastructure in OECD countries*, Edinburgh: Utilities Policy pp. 142-153, 2010
3 Lisa Smith and Lawrence Haddad, *Explaining Child Malnutrition in Developing Countries*, Washington DC: IFPRI, 2000
4 M De Onis et al., *Prevalence thresholds for wasting and stunting in children under five years*, Public Health and Nutrition, pp. 175-179, 2019
5 Ruxin J, *United Nations Protein Advisory Group*, New York: 2013
6 Dr Cicely Wiliams, *Milk and murder*, Speech to Singapore Rotary Club, https://wellcomecollection.org/works/kvffwbrx
7 Jennifer Tappan, *The Riddle of Malnutrition- the long arc of Biomedical and Public Health*, Athens, Ohio: Ohio University Press, 2017
8 John Nott, *How Little Progress?A Political Economy of Post Colonial Nutrition*, Population and Development Review, pp. 771-791, 2018
9 South African Early Childhood Review, *Stunting – a largely invisible condition that is starving Africa's children's potential*, Cape Town, pp. 109-112, 2017
10 United Nations, *Africa Human Development Report 2012 Towards a Food Secure Future*. No. 267636. New York: UNDP, 2012.
11 WHO, *World Health Statistics – Monitoring Health for the SDGs*, NewYork: WHO, 2018
12 UNICEF, WHO, WB, *Levels and Trends in Child Malnutrition*, New York: UNICEF, WHO, WB, 2020

13　UNICEF, *Improving Child Malnutrition, The achievable imperative for global progress*, NewYork: UNICEF, 2013
14　WHO, *World Health Statistics*, New York, 2020
15　Tamara Giles-Vernick and James Webb Jr, *Global Health in Africa*, Athens Ohio: OUP, 2013
16　John Iliffe, *Africans – History of a Continent*, Cambridge: CUP, 2007
17　Basil Davidson, *The Search for Africa – A history in the making*, Oxford: James Currey, 1994
18　The neglected crisis of undernutrition: Evidence for action London, DfID ,2009

Chapter 2
1　Brazelton & Greenspan, *The Irreducible Needs of Children*, Seattle; Amazon, 2000
2　Ferguson Niall, *How Britain Made the Modern World*, London: Penguin Books, 2003
3　John Darwin, *Unfinished Empire*, London: Allen Lane, pp. 1-13, 2012
4　Walter Rodney, *How Europe Underdeveloped Africa*. Nairobi:Pambazuka Press, 1972.
5　Richard Reid and John Parker, *African Histories – Past, Present, and Future*, Oxford: OUP, Handbook of Modern African History, 2013
6　Sethnam Sangera, *Empireland – How Imperialism has Shaped Modern Britain*, London: Penguin, 2021
7　https://www.theguardian.com/politics/2020/jun/12/we-cannot-edit-our-past-boris-johnsons-statue-tweets-explained, 2020
8　*Race and Ethnic Disparities*, London: HMSO, 2021
9　UN Special rapporteur, *Falsifying historical facts may license further racism and discrimination*, London: 2021
10　Jack Woddis, *Africa, the roots of revolt*, London: Lawrence and Wishart, 1960
11　Julius K. Nyerere, *Freedom and Unity: Uhuru na Umoja*, London: OUP, 1967

Chapter 3
1　Eric Williams, *Capitalism and Slavery*, North Carolina: Chapel Hill, 1943
2　Engels Friedrich, *The Working Class in England (1845)*, Leipzig, reprinted London: OUP pp. 36-38, 1999
3　David Olusoga, *First Contacts – the Cult of Progress*, London: Profile Books, pp. 35-50, 2018
4　https://archive.org/stream/in.ernet.dli.2015.201185/2015.201185.The-Book_djvu.txt.
5　Mungo Park, *Travels in the Interior Districts of Africa*, London: JohnMurray, 1799
6　John Iliffe, *The African Poor – A History*, Cambridge: CUP, 1987
7　Culotta E., *Roots of Racism*, Washington DC: Science, 336, pp. 825-827, 2012
8　S.D. Smith, *Slavery, Family and Gentry capitalism in the British Atlantic – the World of the Lascelles 1648-1834*, Cambridge: CUP, 2006

9   Nicholas Rogers, *Murder on the Middle Passage*, London: The Boydell Press, 2020
10 Elikia M'bokolo, *Atlantic Slavery – engendering the racism and contempt from which Africans still suffer*, Paris: Le Monde Diplmatique, 1998
11 William Pettigrew, *Freedom's Debt – The Royal Africa Company and the Politics of the Atlantic Slave trade, 1672-1752*, Williamsburg, Virginia: Chapel Hill, 2013
12 https://www.theguardian.com/world/2020/jun/30/belgian-king-philippe-expresses-profound-regrets-for-brutal-colonial-rule.
13 Mullen S, *Henry Dundas: A 'Great Delayer' of the Abolition of the Transatlantic Slave Trade*, The Scottish Historical Review, Vol 100 (2), pp. 218-248, 2012
14 Melanie Newton, *Children of Africa in the Colonies: Free People of Color in Barbados in the Age of Emancipation – Antislavery, Abolition, and the Atlantic World*, Baton Rouge: LSU Press, 2008
15 Michael Taylor, *The Interest- How the British Establishment Resisted the Abolition of Slavery* London: The Bodley Head, pp. 310-311, 2020
16 Manning P., *Contours of Slavery and Social Change in Africa*, The American Historical Review, Vol 88 No 4 pp. 835-837, 1983
17 Philip D. Curtin, *Measuring the Atlantic Slave Trade*, Cambridge: CUP (online), 2009
18 Lovejoy P. *Transformations in Slavery- a History of slavery in Africa*, Cambridge: CUP, 2012
19 Livingstone op. cit.
20 Bertocchi G., *The legacies of slavery in and out of Africa*, IZA Journal of Migration, 2016
21 M'baye, *The Economic, Political and Social Impact of the Atlantic Slave Trade on Africa*, The European Legacy, 11(6), pp. 607-622, 2006
22 Trevor-Roper H., *Unrewarding African History Gyrations or New Perspectives* https://www.jstor.org/stable/pdf/492770.pdf
23 Davidson B., *The search for Africa's past*, in The Search for Africa London: James Currey, pp. 21-41, 1994

Chapter 4

1 Paul du Chaillu, *Explorations and Adventures in Equatorial Africa 1861*. London: Facsimile Publisher, Chapter 2, 2017
2 Mary S. Lovell, *A Rage to Live, a biography of Richard and Isobel Burton*, London: Little, Brown, 1998
3 Darwin D., *The Descent of Man (1871)*, London, reprinted Wordsworth Editions. 2013
4 Conrad J., *The Heart of Darkness*, London: Blackwoods, 1899
5 Achebe C. *An Image of Africa: Racism in Conrad's Heart of Darkness, Massachusetts Review*, pp. 782-794, 1977
6 https://en.wikipedia.org/wiki/Role of Christianity in civilization

7. https://dokumen.pub/good-economics-for-hard-times-1stnbsped-1541762878-9781541762879.html.
8. Engels, op. cit.
9. Henry Morton Stanley: The 1875 "Daily Telegraph …" http://jonathan-musere.over-blog.com/article-henry-morton-stanley-the-1875-daily-telegraph-recommendation-letter-for-uganda-124866171.html,
10. Hochschild, *King Leopold's Ghost: A Story of Greed, Terror, and Heroism in Colonial Africa*, London: Pan, 1998
11. Jules Marchal, *Lord Leverhulme's Ghosts-Colonial exploration in the Congo*, London: Verso, 2017
12. Brian Lewis, *So Clean – Lord Leverhulme, Soap and Civilization*.Manchester: Manchester UP, pp. 221-222, 2008
13. Caroline Elkins, *Imperial Reckoning – the untold story of Britain's Gulag in Kenya*, New York: Owl Books, 2005
14. Andrea Pitzer, *One Long Night*, New York: Little, Brown, 2015
15. David Olusoga and Casper Erichsen, *The Kaiser's Holocaust – Germany's forgotten Genocide*, London: Faber & Faber, 2011
15. Schweitzer Albert, *My Life and Thought*, London: George Allen and Unwin, 1933
16. Fritz Fanon, *The Wretched of the Earth*, London: Penguin, 1963
17. Georges Nzongola- Ntalaja, *The Congo from Leopold to Kabila; a People's History*, London: Zed Books, 2002
18. Packenham T., *The Scramble for Africa*, London: Weidenfeld and Nicolson, 1991

Chapter 5

1. Kwame Nkrumah, *Neo-Colonialism The last stage of Imperialism*, London: Panaf, 1965
2. Mark Langan, *Neo-Colonialism and the Poverty of 'Developmental in Africa*, London: Springer, 2018
3. Padraig Carmody, *The New Scramble for Africa*, London: Polity, 2016

Chapter 6

1. Service M. W. and Ford J., *The role of Trypanosomiasis in African Ecology*, Journal of Applied Ecology, 1971
2. Kjekshus H. J., *Ecology Control and Economic Development in East African History*. Berkeley & Los Angeles: University of California Press, 1977
3. Pratik Chakrabarti, *Medicine & Empire: 1600–1960*, Social History of Medicine, 28(1), pp. 197-198, 2015
4. Cueto M., *The Origins of Primary Health Care and Selective Primary Health Care*, American Journal of Public Health, 94(11), pp 1864-1874, 2004
5. *Oxford Handbook of Tropical Medicine*, Oxford University Press (2021)
6. Cicely Williams op. cit.

7   Baumslag N., *Primary Health Care Pioneer- The Selected Works of Dr Cicely Williams*, Geneva: WFPHA, UNICEF, 1986
8   Clegg K.M. and Dean R.F.A., *Balance studies on peanut biscuit in the treatment of kwashiorkor*, American Journal of Clinical Nutrition, pp. 885-895, 1960
9   WHO, *Management of severe acute malnutrition in infants*, https://www.who.int/elena/titles/full_recommendations/sam_management/en/.
10 Munro E., The Munro review of child protection: a child-centred system, London: HMSO, 2011
11 Reinhardt, K. and Fanzo, J., *Addressing chronic malnutrition through multi-sectoral, sustainable approaches: a review of the causes and consequences*. Frontiers in Nutrition, 10, pp. 13-13, 2014
12 Iliffe John, *East African Doctors – A History of the Modern Profession*, Cambridge: CUP, 1998
13 Segall, M. *The Politics of Health in Tanzania*, Development and Change, 4(1), pp. 39–50, 1973

Chapter 7

1   For example, and with particular reference to Africa, see Morsink, Johannes. *The universal declaration of human rights*. University of Pennsylvania Press, 2010
2   Newell, K.W., *Health by the people*, Geneva: WHO, 1975
3   Cueto, M., *The Origins of Primary Health Care and Selective Primary Health Care*. American Journal of Public Health, 94(11), pp. 1864-1874, 2004
4   Robert S. McNamara, *One Hundred Countries, Two Billion People – the Dimensions of Development*, New York: Praegar Publishers, 1973
5   Walsh, J. A., Walsh, J. A., Warren, K. S. & Warren, K. S., *Selective primary health care: An interim strategy for disease control in developing countries*. Social Science & Medicine. Part C: Medical Economics, 14(2), pp. 145-163
6   Bell D., *Introduction – post Bellagio Conference*, London: Pergamon Press, Soc. Sci. & Med., Vol. 14C, pp. 63-65, 1980
7   *Improving child nutrition: the achievable imperative for global progress*, UNICEF New York, 2013
8   King, N. B., *Security, Disease, Commerce Ideologies of Postcolonial Global Health*, Social Studies of Science, 32(5), pp. 763-789, 2002
9   Kassalow, J. S., *Why Health is important to U.S. foreign relations*, New York: Council on Foreign Relations and Millbank Memorial Fund, 2001
10 Magnussen, L., Ehiri, J. and Jolly, P., *Comprehensive versus selective primary health care: Lessons for global health policy – Meeting people's basic health needs requires addressing the underlying social, economic, and political causes of poor health*, Health Affairs, 23(3), pp. 167–176, 2004
11 Hall, John and Taylor, R., *Health for all beyond 2000: the demise of the Alma-Ata Declaration and primary health care in developing countries – PubMed – NCBI, Medical Journal of Australia*. pp. 17-20, 2003
12 Brosch Rebecca, op.cit.

13 Xiaoping Fang, *Barefoot Doctors and Western Medicine in China*, Rochester NY: University of Rochester Press, 2012
14 Munroe op. cit.
15 Coile, A., Wun, J., Kothari, M.T., Hemminger, C., Fracassi, P. and Di Dio, D., Scaling up nutrition through multisectoral planning: An exploratory review of 26 national nutrition plans. *Maternal & Child Nutrition*, 17(4), pp. 132-125, 2001.
16 Bergeron, Gilles and Tony Castleman, "Program responses to acute and chronic malnutrition: divergences and convergences," *Advances in Nutrition* 3, no. 2 (2012), pp. 242-249
17 Ooms et al., *The Lancet Commission on Global Governance for Health*, London: The Lancet, vol 383, pp. 636-667, 2014
18 Chan, M., *'Primary Health care is the key to health development and community health security. It works. This is the only way to ensure sustainable access to essential care across a population. We have the evidence'*. WHO global conference, 2011
19 *World Health Statistics – Monitoring Health for the SDGs*, Geneva: WHO, pp. 80-81, 2021
20 Farmer, P., *Pathologies of Power, Human Rights and the New War on the Poor*, Berkeley LA: University of California Press, 2005
21 Crisp, N., *Turning the World Upside Down – The Search for Global Health in the 21st Century*, New York: CRC Press, 2010
22 Farmer, P., *Reimagining Global Health*, Berkeley LA: University of California Press, 2013
23 Litsios Socrates, *The Long and Difficult Road to Alma-Ata: A Personal Reflection*, International Journal of Health Services, 2002
24 Michael Marmot, *The Health Gap – The Challenge of an Unequal World*, London: Bloomsbury, 2015
25 Joseph E. Stiglitz, *The Price of Inequality – How today's Divided Society Endangers Our Future*, New York: W.W.Norton, 2012
26 Wilkinson, R. and Picket, K., *The Spirit Level – Why Equality is Better for Everyone*, London: Penguin, 2010

Chapter 8
1 Ingwe R. et al., *The New Scramble for Africa*, Journal of Sustainable Development, 2010
2 Clare H., *A Single Swallow- Cameroon*, pp. 145-176, London: Vintage, 2010
3 Wiegratz J., *Uganda, the Dynamics of Neoliberal Transformation*, London: Zed, 2018
4 Moyo, D., *Why Foreign Aid Is Hurting Africa*, New York: Wall Street Journal, pp. 1-6, 2009
6 Bush Ray, *Poverty and Neoliberalism: Persistence and reproduction in the Global South*, London: Pluto Press, 2007
8 Kaplinsky, R., *Globalisation, Poverty and Inequality*, London: Polity, 2005

Chapter 9
1. *Global Nutrition Report*, Washington DC: International Food Policy Research Institute, 2015
2. Chambi Chachage and Annar Cassam, *Africa's Liberation – The Legacy of Julius Nyerere*, Kampala; Pambazuka Press, 2010

Chapter 10
1. Kampman, H. et al., *How Senegal created an enabling environment for nutrition: A story of change*, Global Food Security, pp. 57–65, 2017
2. Kanyuka, M., Ndawala, J., Mleme, T. et al., *Malawi and Millennium Development Goal 4: a Countdown to 2015 country case study*, Lancet Global Health, 2016
3. Thomson, Dana et al., *Impact of a health service strengthening system on maternal and child health outcomes in rural Rwanda (2005-2010)*, BMJ, 2018
4. Ambelet, A.A., *Examining changes in child and maternal health in Ethiopia*, International Journal for Equity in Health, 20, pp. 1-16, 2017
5. Azevedo, M.J., *The state of health system(s) in Africa: challenges and opportunities*. In *Historical Perspectives on the State of Health and Health Systems in Africa, Volume II* (pp. 1-73), Palgrave Macmillan, Cham, 2017
6. Omaswa, F. and Crisp, N., *African Health Leaders – Making Change and Claiming the Future*, Oxford: OUP, 2014

Chapter 11
1. Danaei, G. et al., *Risk Factors for Childhood Stunting in 137 Developing Countries: A Comparative Risk Assessment Analysis at Global, Regional, and Country Levels*, PLoS medicine, 2016
2. Finnegan, R., *Time for the World to Learn from Africa*, London; BalestierPress, 2018

This book is printed on paper from sustainable sources managed under the Forest Stewardship Council (FSC) scheme.

It has been printed in the UK to reduce transportation miles and their impact upon the environment.

For every new title that Matador publishes, we plant a tree to offset CO_2, partnering with the More Trees scheme.

MORE TREES
LET'S PLANT A BILLION TREES

For more about how Matador offsets its environmental impact, see www.troubador.co.uk/about/